—PEOPLE TO KNOW—

MARIAN WRIGHT EDELMAN

Fighting for Children's Rights

Wendie Old

ENSLOW PUBLISHERS, INC.

44 Fadem Road
Box 699
Springfield, N.J. 07081
U.S.A.

P.O. Box 38
Aldershot
Hants GU12 6BP
U.K.

Library of Congress Cataloging-in-Publication Data

Old, Wendie C.
　　Marian Wright Edelman: fighting for children's rights / Wendie Old.
　　　　p. cm. — (People to know)
　　Includes bibliographical references (p.) and index.
　　Summary: A biography of the Afro-American lawyer and social reformer who is known for
her work on behalf of children's rights.
　　ISBN 0-89490-623-2
　　　1. Edelman, Marian Wright—Juvenile literature. 2. Afro-American women—United
States—Biography—Juvenile literature. 3. Afro-American women civil rights
workers—United States—Biography—Juvenile literature. 4. Afro-American women social
reformers—United States—Biography—Juvenile literature. 5. Children's rights—United
States—History—20th century—Juvenile literature. [1. Edelman, Marian Wright.
2. Reformers. 3. Afro-Americans—Biography. 4. Women—Biography. 5. Children's rights.]
I. Title. II. Series.
E185.97.E33053 1995
362.7'092—dc20
　[B]　　　　　　　　　　　　　　　　　　　　　　　　　　95-7508
　　　　　　　　　　　　　　　　　　　　　　　　　　　　CIP
　　　　　　　　　　　　　　　　　　　　　　　　　　　　AC

Printed in the U.S.A.

10 9 8 7 6 5 4 3 2 1

Contents

1 A Hungry Child Influences History . . 5

2 Minister's Daughter 10

3 Jim Crow Versus
   Community Support 20

4 Spelman Was the Right Place for Me . . 32

5 "To Be Effective, You Have to
   Be Prepared" 46

6 Mississippi: The Freedom Summer
   of 1964 and Beyond 55

7 Washington, D.C.—Peter and Family . 65

8 The Children's Defense Fund 76

9 A Voice for Children 90

10 "Service Is the Rent
   You Pay for Living" 101

Chronology 111

For Further Information 113

Chapter Notes 114

Further Reading 125

Index 126

Marian Wright Edelman

1

A Hungry Child
Influences History

In the spring of 1967, Senators Robert Kennedy of New York and Joseph Clark of Pennsylvania explored the backwoods dirt roads of the Mississippi Delta area, talking to people and looking into their refrigerators. With them came their aides, followed by a few television camera operators with all their equipment.

Why did these senators leave their comfortable offices in Washington, D.C., to tour this mosquito-infested area? They came because Marian Wright, often called the "fastest-talking woman in the world,"[1] had challenged them to see hunger and poverty in the United States face to face.

These senators were part of the United States Senate's Subcommittee on Employment, Manpower, and Poverty, which had held hearings on the poverty issue in Jackson,

Mississippi. As the lawyer and general counsel for the Child Development Group of Mississippi, Wright testified before this committee. She told them, in her high-speed, soft-spoken way, of the terrible poverty in the Mississippi Delta area. She asked the committee not to stop at listening to the descriptions of the suffering and empty cupboards but to come down and see it for themselves. And she offered to be their guide.

Two of the four senators on the committee accepted her challenge—Senator Robert Kennedy and Senator Joseph Clark. Peter Edelman, one of the men on Senator Kennedy's staff, worked with Wright each day arranging the itinerary.

Marian Wright led them into people's homes—the shacks and shanties of the Delta area. The senators sat and talked with the families. They asked the people to describe what they normally had for breakfast, what they had for dinner. Often the family would invite the group to examine the small portions of food in their refrigerator.

The senators discovered these were people reduced to begging for work. And there was no work for them. They had to beg for food to feed their children. They could not afford medical care. These were people who had to live in dirt floor shanties without running water, lights, heat in the cold winter, or air conditioning in the hot, steaming summer.

Senator Kennedy was particularly disturbed by the situation of one child in Cleveland, Mississippi.

Candidates for public office meet lots of children as they campaign throughout their own states. Schoolchildren sometimes give them letters and flowers. Preschoolers smile and wave. Kennedy could walk up to the shyest child and, within a few moments of fatherly jollying, entice a smile to shine on that child's face.

But this child in the starving, poverty-stricken depths of the Delta was different. He sat listlessly on the dirt floor of the shanty. He did not have the strong, tight muscles of a healthy child. Thin arms and legs were attached to a body that had the swollen belly of a person who has eaten too little food for too long. When a person is in this condition, stomach muscles become weak and the belly sags outwards.

A healthy child would have been curious about all the workings of the strangers with the TV cameras who had invaded his home. Not this child.

During a break, Kennedy sat down by the child and tried to get a response of some sort. But the child just sat there with a blank expression on his face. Kennedy could not elicit any reaction at all.

Marian Wright observed that the plight of that one small child appeared to make Kennedy more angry than anything else she had shown him. Senator Kennedy went back to Washington, D.C., determined to fight for laws to end hunger in the United States of America.

That trip through the Mississippi Delta area changed more than Robert Kennedy's life. It also changed the life

After his fateful trip with Marian Wright, Robert Kennedy testified before a committee in Congress on the plight of the people in Mississippi.

of Marian Wright. She had been fighting for several years as the general counsel for the Child Development Group of Mississippi to make life better for children (and their families) in Mississippi. When she saw how this starving child had affected the powerful Senator Kennedy, she realized that to break the local poverty cycle in Mississippi she had to learn to work with the lawmakers in the national political arena—in the federal government in Washington, D.C.

Within the national arena, she could fight for disadvantaged children everywhere. "It became clear to me that the poor needed a voice in Washington, just like General Motors and other big interests have,"[2] she said.

She had just discovered the key to getting the attention of the lawmakers. It is hard for members of Congress to imagine poverty and starvation as concepts. But if she could show them one starving child . . . could let them see into the refrigerators and empty cupboards of the disadvantaged . . . then they *must* understand the needs of these children and would support laws to help them.[3]

The other change in Marian Wright's life concerned Senator Kennedy's aide, Peter Edelman. "We often say we got together over hungry kids,"[4] she explains, remembering those days fondly. The couple married on July 14, 1968.

She had found her life's work *and* her life-long partner.

2

Minister's Daughter

Marian Wright Edelman grew up surrounded by Baptist ministers. Her grandfather and father were ministers. Her nephew and one of her brothers are now Baptist ministers.

As a result, it should not be surprising that she has spent her life practicing her Baptist beliefs. She remembers that "Service [to others] was as essential a part of my upbringing as eating and sleeping and going to school."[1] This guideline has been the firm underlying fiber weaving through and supporting everything she does.

But before she discovered the best way she could help poor people, especially children in the United States, she took the time to get the right education and training.

Her father, Arthur Jerome Wright, had often said, "You gotta be prepared before you can accomplish anything. You don't settle for anything less than the best."[2]

He knew this from experience. When he returned to his home in Gaffney, South Carolina, after being discharged from the army in 1918 after World War I, he announced to his family that he believed God wanted him to preach. In those days, a person could begin preaching in a church right away, without any training at a seminary.

But Arthur Wright's sister, Marian's Aunt Amma McRee, scoffed at the idea. She had been to college and by the end of the war was earning a living as a teacher. "Who are you going to preach to?" she asked. "Not to me. I've been to school. YOU have to go to school to preach to me." She believed that an untrained preacher would get very little respect in the community. She told him (and later told his children), "It can't be all out of your experience. You have to read and go places. To be effective, you have to be prepared."[3]

Arthur Wright took his sister's advice. He went to college to get some training. While studying at Morris College, a small Baptist college in Sumter, South Carolina, he met a young woman from Spartanburg, South Carolina, who was equally committed to community service. Her name was Maggie Leola Bowen. They married. For the rest of his life, he affectionately called her his "pal" and his "buddy."[4]

Most of the Bowen family had moved North to escape the oppression of the segregated South. Some of Arthur's family had also moved North. But when the African-American Baptist church in the small South

Carolina town of Bennettsville asked them to come serve their community, the couple never hesitated.

Arthur and Maggie Wright worked hard to build the Shiloh Baptist Church congregation and to help the African-American community there. Soon they were acknowledged as strong leaders in their community.

They had five children. Their first child, Olive Wright, was in high school when the last one, Marian Wright, was born on June 6, 1939. In between the two girls came three boys: Arthur, Harry, and Julian Wright.

Marian's sister Olive (now Olive Wright Covington) remembers, "If I wanted to go for a walk to see the boys, I had to take my baby sister. What a bummer!"[5]

But Arthur and Maggie Wright did not stop with caring for their own children. They also eventually cared for about a dozen foster children who needed a home for a while because their own parents were unable to care for them. All of these children were supported by the few dollars a minister earns.

Arthur Wright believed his children should look toward African-American role models. Marian was named after the famous opera singer, Marian Anderson, and was taken to hear her perform when she was old enough to appreciate it.

All of the Wright children were raised on a regimen of study, discipline, self-development, and unceasing service to others. They were brought up to believe that "service is the rent we pay for living."[6]

Her father believed in Booker T. Washington's self-help philosophy: helping others by giving them work to help themselves. He applied this daily within the African-American community of Bennettsville.

The Shiloh Baptist Church congregation was a conservative church group. The choir did not sing gospel music. Marian remembers:

> When I had gotten into the civil rights movement [in the 1960s] and came home and played 'We Shall Overcome' with a jazzy tune, my mother was very disapproving. My daddy was a teacher, and he never trusted a lot of emotion, and I very seldom remember him ever raising his voice on the pulpit.[7]

All of the Wright children were taught music. They received voice and piano lessons to be able to perform for church or Sunday school. Music has remained a source of calm and inspiration throughout Marian's life.[8]

Arthur and Maggie Wright shared in the care of their children. Chores were done *with* the children. Whether it was cleaning house or visiting the sick and poor, the children accompanied their parents as they moved through the day. They learned that nothing was too lowly to do.

Her parents were a strong team—her father the preacher and teacher and her mother the church organizer and fundraiser. Marian Wright Edelman later said:

> Daddy could not have kept the church solvent without her fundraising. She always had a dime squirreled away for crisis, ran her own dairy for a while, and was never without an idea about how to manage in a crunch. . . . [As a result] I have always wanted to earn my own dime.[9]

13

The Wrights expected their children to get an education and to use it to serve their community. The Wright children used to believe their father stayed up all night thinking of jobs to do just to make sure they would not have an idle moment to themselves.

Marian Wright Edelman remembers, "The only time our father would not give us a chore ('Can't you find something constructive to do?' was his most common refrain) was when we were reading. So we all read a lot!"[10]

"The only bad thing about that is that none of us learned how to relax," she recalls.[11]

The children were not even allowed a day off from school assignments. If their father discovered they had no homework that night, he would say, "Well, assign yourself."[12] It took special permission to do anything recreational during the week, because weekdays were to be devoted to school. And school nights were reserved for homework.

But the movie houses in the 1940s showed cowboy serials every Tuesday and Friday evening. If the Wright children saw the beginning of the serial on Friday, how could they get to see the next installment of it on the following Tuesday? The older children tried to convince their parents by pleading that the teachers thought it was educational and had assigned the movies as homework.

But if that did not work, the older children would instruct baby sister Marian to cry. Their parents could resist the tears of the older children, but Mama could not resist

The congregation of Shiloh Baptist Church in Bennettsville was a conservative church group.

Marian's tears. And she could cry instantly, on cue,[13] her sister remembers. Marian was their passport to the movies. In that way, they occasionally got to see werewolves and all the other things that played in the movies during the week.

As the youngest of five, Marian was a special baby, loved by the whole family. By the time most of the older children were off at college, Marian had her parents all to herself. Her father nicknamed her "Booster," because her bubbling personality gave him a boost.[14]

She was smart, too. Although her brother Julian was four or five grades ahead of her, Marian would help him with his homework. She was a well-rounded child. She had lots of friends and was well-liked by the other kids. She was a pretty girl with an outgoing personality.

Although she was a tiny four-year-old when Olive went to Fisk University in Nashville, Tennessee, it was always Marian's goal to follow in her sister's footsteps.[15] In high school, she took all academic courses. In addition to her outside school activities, which included being a drum majorette with the band, and her involvement with church and community, she excelled in school.

Her father believed that "being poor was no excuse for not achieving; and that extra intellectual and material gifts brought with them the privilege and responsibility of sharing with others less fortunate."[16] He would give whole sermons centering around the theme "poverty of things is no excuse for poverty of will and spirit."

Marian Wright is seen here as a young child with her family (left to right, front row) Marian and her friend Ruth; (left to right, back row) Olive, her mother (Maggie), Harry, her father (Arthur), and Julian.

Marian Wright, age seven or eight, poses with her Brownie troop (front row, second from right).

The Wright family had very little money. They never thought of themselves as poor, however, because compared to the people around them, they were not. It was not until years later that she understood what her father was really saying when she would ask for money and her father would reply that he could not give her any because he did not have change for a twenty. There was no twenty dollar bill in his pocket. He did not have any money in his pocket at all. Marian recalls:

> I don't think Daddy ever made more than $200 a month, but it never occurred to us that we were poor. We learned that our worth was measured by what was in our heads and hearts, not by material possessions.[17]

The Wright family was very close. But when her family was not around, Marian found herself under the watchful eye of the members of the congregation and the African-American community who considered themselves her extended family, reporting when she strayed from the straight and narrow of the community expectations and basking in and supporting her achievements when she did well.

All people need community support to face the hardships of life, but African-Americans in the 1940s and 1950s had a special need for it. They also had to live with the horrors of segregation.

3

Jim Crow Versus Community Support

Although Marian grew up protected by her family and her community, she could not avoid the poisonous effects of segregation. Before she could read, Marian learned that "white only" signs meant she was not welcome.

It was difficult for a thirsty African-American five-year-old to understand why she must not drink from the water fountain in a downtown department store. Why should the fact that the color of her skin was darker than some other people's in town matter? But the neighbor who had taken her to the store scolded her and dragged the still thirsty child away.

She hated being excluded. Even to this day she cannot stand being excluded from anything.[1]

Many children enjoy sitting in the balcony of a movie house, but in Bennettsville and throughout many of the southern states, all of the African-American people were required to sit there. They were forbidden to sit on the main floor. The main floor was for white people only. When Marian became old enough to realize what was happening, she felt humiliated. "There was never a time I didn't know segregation was wrong,"[2] Marian recalled.

She and her friends could not swim in the town's public pool, even though it was practically across the street from her home. They had to swim in a nearby creek or in the river at the edge of town. She later learned that part of the creek where they swam and fished was below the hospital sewage outlet.

Poor people could not get medical attention. It became especially difficult if they were both poor and African American. For instance, a boy who lived near her home once stepped on a nail. The puncture wound later became infected, and the boy died. No one knows if he died from tetanus or another side effect of the infection, because no doctor ever saw him. The boy's grandmother had no money to pay for health care.

Marian will never forget the terrible accident on the highway that runs right in front of her childhood home. A black migrant family's car collided with a truck driven by a white man. Only one ambulance arrived. The ambulance driver examined the white truck driver, declared him unhurt, and drove off. He refused to do anything for the badly injured black victims. After all, his ambulance was a "white" ambulance; he did not carry black people, no matter how badly injured they were. He left them lying on the road. "I remember watching children like me bleeding," she recalls, "I remember the ambulance driving off. You never, ever forget."[3] Incidents like this just drove her "wild."[4]

She and every other African American were forced to endure these episodes of discrimination because of laws enacted in the 1880s and 1890s after the Civil War. These laws, often called Jim Crow laws, were meant to "keep the Negro in his place; to make him constantly aware that he was not the equal of any white man."[5] This gave whites someone to look down on and made the blacks feel inferior.

The term Jim Crow referred to a blackface character (a white man with the black from burnt-cork smeared on his face) in a minstrel show of the 1830s. The character performed a song and dance routine called "Jump Jim Crow."[6] This song became associated with segregation.

There was no official law enforcing segregation in the South before the Civil War—just social custom. Black slaves, white masters, freedmen, and freedwomen mingled almost freely because most everyone knew their own status in life and were aware of the invisible social lines that they could not cross. After the war, a series of "Black Codes" were enacted mostly by the Southern states to make certain that the newly freed slaves would remain in a slavelike condition.

Several amendments to the United States Constitution attempted to strike down the Black Codes and insure the newly freed slaves' rights. The Fourteenth Amendment of 1868 stated that all citizens were entitled to an equal protection of the laws of the land. The Fifteenth Amendment of 1870 stated that the right of citizens to vote could not be denied because of race or color or because the person used to be a slave.

Finally in 1896, the Supreme Court decision in *Plessy* v. *Ferguson* sparked a reaction throughout the South to officially segregate the blacks and whites. This decision ruled that all railroad companies must provide equal but separate accommodations for the white and black races.[7]

Many states (mostly Southern states) used this ruling to amend their Black Codes with a strict interpretation of the separate but equal parts of the law. However, it proved almost impossible to provide two of everything and keep the quality high on both. It also proved impossible to keep them equal. Since the whites held much more economic power than blacks, their equal share of things—from park benches to education—somehow came out more equal than the share for blacks.

People called these new laws Jim Crow laws. They made it illegal for blacks to use white-designated street cars, railroad cars, restrooms, schools, parks, restaurants, and water fountains. These laws also often affected the

Separate doors for whites and blacks were a familiar part of life in the South under the "Jim Crow" laws.

town's zoning laws, forcing blacks to accept the poorest housing.

While Jim Crow laws were not limited to the South, they were more numerous there. In truth, Northern and Western states also had discriminatory laws. The labor unions across the nation refused to let blacks (and other minorities) become members, which effectively relegated them to the pick and shovel jobs or the role of a sharecropper or servant.

Some small areas did not even try to provide equal areas for blacks. This was why Marian and her family and friends often found in the 1940s that they were not allowed to enter parks or even sit in a soda fountain shop sipping a soda.

Even more demeaning was the attitude of many southern whites towards blacks. A South Carolina woman told a Northern teacher in the early 1900s, "You might as well try to teach your horse or mule to read as to teach these . . . ."[8]

The attitude that blacks were dirty, diseased, and dumb prevailed for many years after the Civil War, despite the fact that whites employed blacks as cooks, maids, housekeepers, and wet nurses, especially in South Carolina.

Marian can never forget the ugly voices of her small southern segregated town. She remembers hearing former South Carolina Senator James Byrnes roaring to a gathering on the courthouse lawn, just a few blocks from her house, declaring that black children would never go to school with whites.

Few whites wanted to attend the black schools in the South. School boards were usually made up of white people. The buildings allocated to the blacks by the white school board were often substandard with unheated classrooms. The textbooks allocated to some southern black schools were falling apart, and since not enough were sent for each class, the students often had to share.

American society told the black children of the 1940s and 1950s that they were not as important as whites. But Marian maintains that "We were never hopeless and we never despaired because we had [caring and courageous] adults out there struggling with us, being there for us, and buffering us"[9] from this negative attitude. "Our parents said it wasn't so, our teachers said it wasn't so, and our preachers said it wasn't so."[10] "They believed in us, and we, therefore, believed in ourselves."[11]

Because there was no public playground where black children were allowed to play, Reverend Wright built one behind the church, complete with a merry-go-round. Because there was no place for black teenagers to hang out, Reverend Wright established a canteen for all blacks behind the church.

Wherever Marian's father saw a need, he responded. Marian never forgot the lesson that "if you don't like the way the world is, you change it. You have an obligation to change it. You just do it, one step at a time."[12]

There was no home in Bennettsville for elderly African Americans too poor to live on their own. In response to that need, her father and mother established the Wright Home for the Aged, at first in a house across the street from the church and later in a brick home behind the church. The entire Wright family, even the smallest children, helped cook and serve and clean the home and the people who lived in it.

Marian often tells people, "Helping other people, I did it as a kid like other kids go to the movies. It is what I was raised to be."[13]

Nationally, in the early 1950s, an important court case was wending its way up to the Supreme Court— *Brown* v. *the Board of Education of Topeka, Kansas.* Five cases were included under this title. Possibly because one of the five cases under consideration came from Clarendon County, South Carolina, Marian's father often discussed the importance of it with her and how it might affect the lives of African Americans in the United States. This case would overrule the *Plessy* v. *Ferguson* decision. African Americans everywhere, including the Wrights, hoped it would end the reign of the "separate but equal" Jim Crow laws.

Reverend Wright never lived to hear the decision. In the spring of 1954, he suffered a heart attack. When he felt the chest pains, he spoke of going away, his work for

Marian's parents founded the Wright Home for the Aged across the street, later building this brick house behind the church in Bennettsville which is now dedicated to her mother.

the Lord finished on this earth. Fourteen-year-old Marian rode with him in the ambulance. His last words to her were, "Booster, don't let anything get in the way of your education."[14] He died before the ambulance reached the hospital.

In remembering that day, Marian says:

> He had holes in his shoes but two children out of college, one in college, another in divinity school, and a vision he was able to convey to me as he lay dying . . . that I, a young Black girl, could be and do anything; that race and gender are shadows and that character, self-discipline, determination, attitude, and service are the substance of life.[15]

Ten days later the landmark U.S. Supreme Court *Brown* v. *the Board of Education of Topeka, Kansas* decision was handed down. It ruled that "Separate educational facilities are inherently unequal. Therefore . . . the plaintiffs . . . are . . . deprived of equal protection of the laws as guaranteed by the 14th Amendment."[16] of the U.S. Constitution.

In May of the next year, 1955, the Court ordered the southern states to desegregate their schools with "all deliberate speed." This order is often called *Brown II.* Unfortunately, they obeyed with all deliberate slowness.

All of the African-American children in the town of Bennettsville and the surrounding areas of Marlboro County, including the Wright children, attended the same school—Marlboro Training School—from grades

All the African-American children in Bennettsville, South Carolina, attended Marlboro Training School. The school went from first to twelfth grade.

one through twelve. These crowded conditions were eased in 1956 with the building of a new black high school—Eastside High School. In the fall of 1956, the ninth through twelfth grades transferred to the new high school. Marian was a member of the last class to graduate from Marlboro Training School. However, the new building was completed in time for her class to hold their graduation ceremonies in its much larger auditorium.

4

Spelman Was the
Right Place for Me

In 1956 when Marian Wright was selecting a college to attend, the family still lived in the Shiloh Church parsonage in Bennettsville. Wright says:

> My mother did not miss a beat in assuming either the family or church leadership mantle. . . . [She] continued as family navigator and glue, church organist and fund-raiser, and nurturer of my father's legacy of service in and outside the home.[1]

When Reverend Wright died, several years earlier, the choice of a new minister appeared logical. The church called Harry Wright home from divinity school to be their minister.

He agreed, on the condition that he could continue his studies. The church worked out a financial arrangement to help him get his degree. He had hoped to find a nearby college where he would be able to continue his studies as well as fulfill the duties of minister at Shiloh Baptist Church. He applied to Duke University, but they rejected him—because they were not taking any black students. This blatant denial of the Supreme Court ruling made him so furious that he wrote a very angry letter to the newspaper.

He ended up going back to Colgate Rochester in New York state, even though the logistics of doing this plus serving as the minister of the church were very trying.[2]

It would be several more years before the major white colleges and universities of the South accepted blacks on their campuses.

Since all her brothers and sisters had gone to college, it never occurred to Marian that she would not attend. She understood she was expected to share what she had learned and earned with the less fortunate as her older brothers and sister had done. But circumstances had changed with her father's death. It was going to be harder to scrape together the college fees.

Marian Wright applied to and was accepted at several colleges. She really wanted to attend the same one her sister, Olive, had attended—Fisk University in Nashville, Tennessee.[3]

However, she was offered a full scholarship to Spelman College in Atlanta, Georgia. Marian declared, "I hated the idea of going to a staid women's college, but it turned out to be the right place for me after all."[4] Her mother and her brother Harry urged her to accept it. "If you're kinda poor and you have to choose, you choose the one where you've got the scholarship," Olive Wright Covington commented. "She loved Spelman and still does."[5]

Spelman College is the largest liberal arts college for African-American women. At that time, it had a very conservative reputation. Students were referred to as *ladies* and were required to wear hats and gloves whenever they went off campus. Early curfews were strictly enforced.

She discovered that the same values her father and mother had stressed about taking responsibility for her own learning and growth were also emphasized in the compulsory daily (except for Saturday) chapel services. If you missed a service, the school could take points off your grade point average. This ensured almost perfect attendance by everyone.

Wright remembers more from the chapel speakers who discussed life and the purpose of education than from any particular class she took. Many of the speakers went on to become nationally famous, including Whitney Young, who became the head of the National Urban League; Carl Holman, who became head of the National Urban Coalition; and Dr. Martin Luther King, Jr., who became a civil rights leader.

It is not surprising that Dr. Martin Luther King, Jr., visited the campus several times during Marian's attendance there, since King's sister taught at Spelman.

Wright says she remembers more from the chapel speakers at Spelman than from any particular class she took. Shown is Sister's Chapel on the Spelman campus.

Marian was impressed by his message but had little idea as to exactly how important he would become to her life.

All these speakers, plus many others, brought the Spelman ladies the same message Wright's father had taught—that education should be used for improving the lives of others and for leaving your community and world better off than you found it.

The family and community support Wright had relied on in Bennettsville continued while she attended college. Her friends and neighbors knew she was on a tight budget. They surprised her with care packages of food and greasy dollar bills stuffed into shoe boxes, carefully tied with string.

Wright chose her course of study to prepare for a career in the foreign service. Therefore whenever she was offered an opportunity to travel, she took it. Her sister, Olive Wright Covington, explains that whenever a letter came home stating that Marian wanted to do this or that, Mom would say, "Let's find the money." No questions asked.[6] One summer Wright went to Africa.

She won a Charles Merrill study/travel grant for study abroad during her junior year. She studied French civilization during the summer at the Sorbonne in Paris, France. In the fall, she decided to move on to the University of Geneva in Switzerland for the academic year.

She had wanted to visit Russia ever since reading the novels of Leo Tolstoy.[7] She had her chance the next

Spelman College is the largest liberal arts college for African-American women. Shown here is Rockefeller Hall.

summer. Operation Crossroads, an exchange program between Soviet Russia and the United States, offered her a Lisle Fellowship to Moscow. She took advantage of the new dialogue the Soviet Premier Nikita Khrushchev had opened up with the Western nations and went on a study-tour. Her mother provided the extra money she needed for this trip by selling a small piece of property she had inherited from her husband. Once there Marian discovered she did not agree with the Soviet system of economics. Marian remembers:

> That year gave me a sense of confidence that I could navigate in the world and do just about anything.[8] It was a great liberating experience. After a year's freedom as a person, I wasn't prepared to go back to a segregated existence.[9]

While Wright had been out of the country, the Civil Rights Movement had really begun to roll.

One of the first major events of the movement had happened while Wright was in high school. On December 1, 1955, in Montgomery, Alabama, a tired black seamstress, Rosa Parks, was asked to give up her bus seat to a white man. She simply said, "No."

Because it was against the Jim Crow laws for a black person to refuse to allow a white person to take his or her seat, Parks was arrested. This time the black community reacted. A group of black community leaders made up of both men and women, including the Reverend Ralph

During her summer in Russia, Marian Wright (second from left) and her companions were able to meet Premier Nikita Khrushchev (third from right).

Abernathy and Dr. Martin Luther King, Jr., organized a black boycott of the Montgomery, Alabama, bus lines.

Suddenly two groups of people learned two different things. The bus company learned that it depended upon the ridership of the blacks in the city to keep its bus company solvent, and black people learned that if they banded together, they could change unfair laws.

The Montgomery, Alabama, city buses were desegregated by court order in December 1956.

But Montgomery, Alabama, seemed very far away from Wright's home in South Carolina and her college in Atlanta, Georgia.

Then on February 1, 1960, four freshmen at the Negro Agricultural and Technical College in Greensboro, North Carolina, bought some school supplies at a five and dime store, then sat at the store's lunch counter and asked politely for coffee and doughnuts. The surprised waitress told them that she was sorry, but "we don't serve you here."[10]

The students objected. They pointed out that the store had just taken their money for school supplies. The cashier had not put their money in a special box marked *black* money. So why should there be a *white only* lunch counter?

They ordered coffee again. The waitress did not serve them. The four young men sat on the lunch counter stools all afternoon and evening until the store closed. They were never served.

Marian Wright described her Russian trip as "a great liberating experience." Here, she pauses to pose in front of the entrance to the University of Moscow.

A new word spread throughout the African-American colleges in the South: SIT-IN. By March 1960, the African-American students of Atlanta began to organize their own sit-ins to expose the Jim Crow injustices.

A sit-in was simply this: The students would locate restaurants who refused to serve African-Americans. Large numbers of the students would enter the restaurant, sitting in every seat at every table and counter. They would sit there for hours quietly trying to order and preventing white people from finding a place to sit.

When the owners called for the police, the students would willingly let themselves be arrested, secure in the knowledge that another group of African-American students were poised to take their seats. Wave after wave of protesters blocked the lunch counters until the jails were full.

The businesspeople were losing money. They were not pleased. The sit-in people were preventing paying customers from using their establishment. White segregationists who wished to patronize the business grew upset themselves about the protesters. Some ignored the students, but others were more violent—yelling, pushing, or even hitting them.

Many of the students had learned a lesson from Mohandas Gandhi's nonviolent protests in India of the 1940s. Those nonviolent protests had finally resulted in

India becoming an independent country instead of a British colony. The students were determined that their sit-ins would also remain a nonviolent protest. This self-discipline created a nationwide respect for their courage and a wave of positive public opinion for their cause.

The movement grew and grew. The term, sit-in, was adapted for other kinds of protests. Large numbers of blacks crowded the all-white pools. This was called a wade-in. Many blacks pushed their way into segregated theaters creating stand-ins. There were also sit-ins at libraries that refused to loan books to blacks, kneel-ins in the pews of all-white churches, and lie-ins on the beds at hotels and motels.

Newly returned from the Soviet Union, Wright decided to jump into the fray. She was convinced that segregation was wrong and was something to be fought against. She volunteered to participate in what was to become one of the largest sit-ins in Atlanta—at the city hall cafeteria. She posted a notice in Spelman's dormitories, encouraging friends to join her: "Young Ladies who can picket, please sign below."[11]

Of all the Spelman students who participated, fourteen were arrested, including Wright. She remembers:

> It never occurred to me NOT to get arrested. I called my mother beforehand and told her what I was going to do, and she didn't object, although I know she was worried.[12]

Maggie Wright did promise she would pray for her daughter and her friends.

Since Wright thought it was very possible that she would be arrested, she brought along a book she had been meaning to read if she ever had the time. She spent the night in jail reading C.S. Lewis's *The Screwtape Letters.*[13]

After the experience at the sit-in, Wright decided to become even more involved in the Civil Rights Movement. She did volunteer work at the local Atlanta office of the NAACP (National Association for the Advancement of Colored People). This was a real eye-opener.

She cataloged discrimination complaints. The huge number of them angered her.[14] "There were so many,"[15] she recalls—so many people who could not afford help. They could not get help because there were so few black lawyers and the majority of Southern white lawyers refused to argue civil rights cases. Wright could see there was an urgent need for black lawyers.

Wright's activities with the protests and the NAACP helped her discover a different life goal than her earlier ambition for a career in the foreign service.

"The years at Spelman expanded her world," her sister, Olive Wright Covington, remembers, "When she graduated (in 1960), she already had a world view and we knew she was going to be extraordinary."[16]

She thought long and hard about her decision. Here she was, poised to go to graduate school. She had intended to major in Russian studies and then apply for a career in the foreign service. The lure of travel and faraway places called to her.

But so many people here in the United States needed lawyers, and there were so few available.

Wright confesses, "I had no aptitude or interest in law. I simply thought about what was needed."[17]

Wright did apply to graduate school, but not in Russian studies. She applied to Yale Law School in New Haven, Connecticut—and was accepted.

She turned her face away from foreign service and committed herself to fill the need for African-American lawyers.

5

"To Be Effective,
You Have to Be Prepared"

Marian Wright graduated from Spelman College in 1960. She could not afford law school any more than she had been able to afford to go to the first four years of college. Therefore she applied for financial aid and was awarded a fellowship. Wright entered Yale as a John Hay Whitney fellow. Her sister, Olive Wright Covington, explains:

> She really didn't have an interest in the law—to be a lawyer or to practice law. But she felt deeply about what was happening and felt somebody had got to go and do something. After all, if you see something that needs to be done, you don't say 'how come somebody doesn't do something?' You say, 'how come *I* don't do something?'...Going to law school put her into the situation as an effective person. Remember, Dad said, 'You gotta be prepared. You don't settle for anything less than the best.'[1]

Marian Wright graduated from Spelman College in 1960. Here, Wright poses in cap and gown with mother (Maggie) to her right, and family and friends to her left.

Wright confesses, "I hated every minute of [law school]. What kept me there was knowing I was needed. . . . "[2]

In the spring of 1960 when Wright was making the decision to become a lawyer, a new black organization was being created.

The Student Non-Violent Coordinating Committee (SNCC) was a small but militant group of students, most of whom had participated in the sit-ins. The membership of the organization was mostly black and became completely black by 1966 as whites were eased (or pushed) out (under the direction of SNCC leader Stokely Carmichael's move to "Black Power"). Even in 1960 when Wright joined, all the leaders of the organization were black.

Although this group had very little money, its members were dedicated. They moved to poor, African-American areas to work and live with the people. They set up Freedom Schools to teach the neighborhood about their voting rights. And they helped register many African Americans to vote.

Being college students, they had learned that the right to vote was the way to power. If you can vote, you can elect a mayor who believes in integration. If you can vote, you can elect a school board who sees that books are in the hands of all the children.

Theoretically the United States Constitution defends the right for every citizen to vote. However, in practice, things were quite different.

In the 1960s, many states still had the old-fashioned poll tax that every prospective voter had to pay. The tax was so high that very poor people, both white and black, could not afford it. (The twenty-fourth Amendment to the Constitution, ratified in 1964, eliminated the poll tax in federal elections.)

Another way to prevent African Americans from voting was the literacy test, first established in Mississippi, then enacted by several other Southern states.

Theoretically, no person could vote who was unable to read and explain the meaning of any section of the U.S. Constitution to the satisfaction of the voter registrars. In practice, registration officials would accept any explanation by a white person, but would disqualify a black no matter what explanation he or she might give.[3]

Even if black persons were registered to vote, the white community had other ways to prevent them from casting their votes.

For example, some polling (voting) places were set up miles away from black communities. If black people had to use a ferry to cross a river to reach their assigned polling place, the ferry might be 'out of order' on election day. Some black voters had to pass a gauntlet of glaring white men carrying guns to get into their polling place. And at times, threats and violence would be aimed at blacks before election day to prevent them from even wishing to vote.

The members of the SNCC tried to help the poor blacks get registered and get to the polling places.

At that time, most of the major civil rights organizations were still committed to the philosophy of nonviolence as preached by Martin Luther King, Jr., who said, "We will soon wear you down by our capacity to suffer and in winning our freedom we will so appeal to your heart and conscience that we will win you in the process."[4]

In 1963, during the spring break of her last year in law school, Wright went to Greenwood, Mississippi, to help the SNCC voter registration drive there. Her friend Robert Moses, the field secretary for the SNCC there, had invited her. (At that time, Mississippi had the largest population of African Americans in the United States and SNCC was gearing up for a big push to register voters there.) Wright recalls:

> The black people had all heard that a lady lawyer (almost) from up North was coming—me. They'd expected to see some well-dressed hotshot, and when I showed up in jeans, I could see they were disappointed. After that, I always tried to look good.[5]

But she discovered that the local white community, including the police, resented these outsiders coming in and educating blacks about their rights.

She knew she only had a short time there because she had to get back to class. She worked diligently the whole week.

On her last day there, she accompanied a march to the voter registration office in Greenwood. They were

In 1963, Marian Wright participated in the SNCC voter registration drive in Greenwood, Mississippi. Here, a Mississippi woman fills out a voter registration form.

met by club-swinging police officers and attacked by German shepherd police dogs.

Wright was angry. "The FBI was standing there and not doing anything. I was so outraged." The police arrested many of the marchers. "I called the lawyers in Jackson [Mississippi]," she remembers, "but they were 100 miles away. I realized how isolated the people [in Greenwood] were—totally at the mercy of local authority."[6]

She never forgot the terror of that spring break. "To this day, if I see a German shepherd on the street, I'll cross over to avoid him."[7]

And she added another reason to the list of why people must be able to vote: If you can vote, you can elect a police commissioner or a sheriff who does not turn attack dogs on children.[8] Wright returned to Yale even more determined to pass the rigorous course load there.

Before she received her LL.B. degree (Bachelor of Laws, a degree all practicing lawyers must have) in May of 1963, she joined the NAACP Legal Defense and Educational Fund. After her graduation, the Fund sent her to be trained at their offices in New York City. While there, she learned how to provide legal assistance for southern blacks in civil rights cases.

By the end of 1963, she knew her father had been right. All this training was forging her into a useful tool to help her people in the South. At the end of her training

On Wright's last day in Greenwood, her group was attacked by police dogs as they marched to the voter registration office. In a similar scene, this photo shows police dogs in Mississippi attacking an unidentified protester on March 29, 1961.

year, she was given a choice of positions—anywhere in the South. She chose Jackson, Mississippi, because it seemed to have the most need. "At [that] time the state had some 900,000 blacks and just three black lawyers."[9] Wright decided to make that four black lawyers.

Her family supported her decision, although naturally her mother worried somewhat.[10] Olive remembers that "by that time we had all come to understand that Marian had her own mind."[11]

But the summer of 1964 was an important event in the civil rights struggle. It was the time of the Mississippi Summer Project. And Marian Wright would find herself fighting in the thick of it.

6

Mississippi: The Freedom Summer of 1964 and Beyond

In the spring of 1964, Marian Wright set off to face the lion's den in Mississippi by opening a branch of the NAACP Legal Defense and Education Fund office in the city of Jackson, the state capitol. Her annual salary of $7,200 was much less than lawyers were getting elsewhere but was higher than teachers and most other college graduates received in Mississippi.

She opened the office just in time. This was the Freedom Summer of 1964, and she was in the middle of the Mississippi Summer Project. The call had gone out throughout the land, and thousands of volunteers, both white and black, students and older working people, single and married, surged into Mississippi to help register black voters.

The whole campaign had been organized by the Council of Federated Organizations (the CoFO), consisting of representatives from CORE (Congress of Racial Equality), SCLC (the Southern Christian Leadership Conference), SNCC, and the NAACP.

Several reports have estimated that during the course of the campaign there were one thousand arrests, thirty-five shooting incidents, thirty buildings bombed, thirty-five churches burned, eighty people beaten, and at least six murdered.[1]

Looking back at that summer, one person from nearby Alabama said, "Progress came through agony."[2]

As for how many African-American voters actually managed to be registered that summer, the exact total is unknown, but many reports say there were only a handful.

However, the CoFO claimed the Mississippi Summer Project succeeded in several important ways. With national publicity exposing the violent emotional reactions of the people in Mississippi to the invasion of the volunteers, it raised the Mississippi blacks to political consciousness, helped develop the Freedom Democratic Party, awakened whites to their responsibilities, and established black leadership.[3]

However the whole event was frightening to live through. Marian Wright often heard bombs exploding, never knowing when one would be aimed at her. She learned never to crank up "my car in the morning without

As seen here, the NAACP was one of the most influential groups in the drive to register Mississippi voters.

leaving the driver's-side door open. That way . . . if a bomb was planted under the hood and exploded, there was a chance of being thrown out and escaping death."[4] She had to learn how to function effectively in spite of living with the fear of being shot at.

She discovered her main job as lawyer for the NAACP was to get these volunteers out of jail. She remembers, "That summer I very seldom got a client out of jail who had not been beaten by a white police officer, who didn't have bones broken and teeth missing."[5]

Sometimes she did not succeed in getting them out of jail in time. "One kid I represented had been killed in jail." She had to take the news to the family and help them through the process of claiming the body:

> I went with the family to take clothes to the undertaker. I remember the sheet being pulled up over this kid and looking at the wound and watching his parents. Something [inside me] just snapped. I had nightmares for a long time.[6]

Depressing events like this would make her despair about the possibility of the law being a viable instrument of the process. "One keeps plugging, trying to make our institutional processes work."[7]

She discovered the most important weapon in her arsenal was the ability to face trouble and stay cool. This way she could effectively help her clients and avoid trouble for herself.

On July 2, President Lyndon B. Johnson signed the Civil Rights Act of 1964, which outlawed segregation in public accommodations. (It was later upheld by the U.S. Supreme Court.) Slowly a body of law was being enacted by the national government that would make Wright's work in Mississippi more effective in terms of being able to help improve the lives of the poor people there.

But she still had a long way to go. After the summer volunteers returned to their homes and schools, she still had thousands of cases to settle. And then there were those people who had registered to vote but had lost their jobs on the plantations—who did not even have the two dollars necessary to buy food stamps.

Wright says, "It became very clear that unless you gave people the social and economic means to exercise those [political and civil] rights," you hadn't succeeded in your purpose.[8]

President Johnson's War on Poverty also went into gear in the year 1964. This massive federal program aimed to rebuild urban neighborhoods and create new jobs for the unemployed. Wright immediately discovered the part of that program most important to her and the people she was trying to help—the part called Head Start.

Project Head Start, launched in 1965, had been set up to serve the needs of the whole family in order to best serve the needs of the poor, preschool child. Beginning as a summer program in 3,300 centers, it initially helped over 550,000 people. Project Head Start called for the establishment of centers in communities across the nation. These centers were to offer education, nutrition, meals, and social and medical services for the families in that locality. It also served to help people help themselves by getting them directly involved in the running of the program.

It seemed as if the money was dangling just out of reach. The national government had the money and had developed the guidelines for the program. All the states had to do was ask for it. But what frustrated Wright the most was that, even though Mississippi's need for Head Start was probably the greatest in the nation, the conservative state politicians, both in Washington, D.C., and at the state level, refused to ask. (At times Wright was convinced the politicians just did not want to help the poor and African-American families. However, there may have been another reason for their hesitation. At that time, the national government only offered start-up monies for Head Start. After a predetermined amount of time, the states were supposed to take over the funding. Since Mississippi was a poor state, the politicians may have been afraid the state budget could not afford it.)

Wright took her bar exam in the spring of 1965. (Every lawyer is required to take this examination for admittance to the state bar association in order to practice law in that state.) When she arrived at the testing area, she discovered she was the only African-American

President Johnson's War on Poverty sought to help those in need. This tar paper shack represents the homes of many in the South in 1964.

person taking the test that day. However, she was pleased to find that "they were astonishingly nice to me."[9] She passed and became the very first African-American woman admitted to the Mississippi State Bar Association.

Wright found helping one person at a time too slow and frustrating. In order to assist large groups of people, that spring she became the lawyer and general counsel for the Child Development Group of Mississippi. This was a federation of religious and civil rights groups (including the Delta Ministry of the National Council of Churches) who combined in an attempt to get federal Head Start funds for the children of Mississippi. Wright thought it was "one of the most exciting educational programs for poor folks in the nation."[10] She could see that Head Start was the embodiment of her father's belief that self-help was the way to the betterment of people. She knew that lifting children from poverty may be the best way to help poor African Americans share in the nation's prosperity.[11]

With Wright's legal help, the Child Development Group of Mississippi managed to dislodge the logjam in the flow of millions of federal dollars, reopening and/or establishing over one hundred Head Start centers in the state.

Writer and educator Robert Coles has said, "It's almost impossible to convey to people what it meant for a black woman to do that in Jackson, Mississippi, in 1965. She has unwavering moral courage."[12]

On August 6, 1965, President Johnson signed into law the Voting Rights Act, which set aside literacy tests and authorized federal examiners to begin registering African Americans in Alabama, Georgia, Louisiana, Mississippi, Virginia, South Carolina, and thirty-four counties of North Carolina.[13] With this federal protection of African-American voting rights, Jim Crow was legally dead.

As the lawyer and general counsel for the Child Development Group of Mississippi, Marian Wright was called to testify before the United States Senate's subcommittee on Employment, Manpower, and Poverty, which held hearings on the poverty issue in Jackson, Mississippi, in 1967. She poured all the experience of her past three years of working with Mississippi's poor into her testimony.

Taking Senators Kennedy and Clark to see and hear for themselves the results of poverty in the people's homes—how it affected children as well as adults—proved to be tremendous eye openers to both the northern senators and to the newspeople accompanying them.

Wright spent every evening during that trip arranging the next day's itinerary with Senator Kennedy's legislative assistant, Peter Edelman, a graduate of Harvard Law and former Supreme Court clerk. The mutual attraction between them might have been like ships passing at sea, never to meet again, except for Wright's own reaction to the events on that trip.

When she saw how the starving child had affected the powerful Senator Kennedy, it came to her that it was not just a local problem—there were disadvantaged children everywhere—and that in order to break the local poverty cycle in Mississippi, it might be necessary to work with the lawmakers in the national political arena—in the federal government in Washington, D.C. Perhaps if the nation's lawmakers learned to understand the needs of these children—of all children—they would support laws to help them.

To reach and influence these lawmakers, she would have to find a way to get to Washington, D.C.

7

Washington, D.C.— Peter and Family

Immediately upon his return to Washington, D.C., Senator Robert Kennedy met with Secretary of Agriculture Orville L. Freeman, urging him to send people to Mississippi to investigate the problem of poverty and hunger and do something to help. In addition, Kennedy made *Hunger in America* one of the major themes of his speeches during his travels throughout the United States as a presidential candidate.

Kennedy sent his assistant, Peter Benjamin Edelman, who was eager to renew his acquaintance with the bright, young, NAACP lawyer, back to Mississippi with the group from the Department of Agriculture.

Wright remembers their courtship, "We shared values. He's a kind man who I thought would also be big enough to let me be me. And that's not easy for somebody, I suspect."[1]

A long-distance romance can be very frustrating. Since she wanted to live near Peter Edelman, Wright applied for, and later that year received, a grant from the Field Foundation to study how to make laws work for the poor. This enabled her to go to Washington, D.C., in March of 1968 and establish the Washington Research Project. The project's goals were to report on the poor and underprivileged throughout the country, to be a voice for America's poor, and to see that the laws that had been enacted to protect them were enforced.

Now both Peter Edelman and Marian Wright had jobs in Washington, D.C., and it seemed like the perfect arrangement. But life never runs as smoothly as you plan. In April 1968, the major spokesperson for the Civil Rights Movement, Dr. Martin Luther King, Jr., was cut down by an assassin's bullet.

No sooner had the nation begun to recover from that shock than the major contender in the race for the presidency was also shot. In an event covered by many TV news cameras, Senator Robert Kennedy walked from a party celebrating his winning another primary election (in California), cut through the kitchen to exit quietly (instead of exiting through the mob of fans at the front of the building), and was gunned down.

In the early 1990s, Marian Wright Edelman was asked by a *Rolling Stone* reporter if she felt there are any modern leaders who would measure up to Robert Kennedy. She replied:

> I have not sensed among many the capacity that he had to deal with the poor blacks and the poor whites and with kids—he had that gift. But I don't go around in my life looking for Robert Kennedy again. Or for Martin King again.[2]

Despite being in mourning for Kennedy, Marian Wright and Peter Edelman decided to go ahead with their plans for a July wedding. Peter Edelman came from a white, conservative Jewish family in Minneapolis, Minnesota. He was three generations removed from Russia, one generation removed from poverty. His grandfather had supported his entire immigrant family from age twelve, beginning with peddling papers on freezing street corners.

For many years, Virginia had laws forbidding interracial marriages. However, the Supreme Court had recently struck them down. Their marriage, July 14, 1968, in the backyard of a friend's house near Washington, D.C., was one of the first interracial marriages in Virginia.

Again, Wright's family supported her choice. The only thing her mother asked was if she had thought carefully about what this would mean. When assured that her daughter was firm in her choice, Wright's mother warmly welcomed Peter Edelman into the family.

But not all African Americans were as forgiving. For a while, there were places where she was not invited. However, since Marian Wright Edelman has been determined all her life to choose the way she wanted to live, she tried not to let it bother her. Edelman says that "what other people thought—whether black or white—didn't have much to do with my basic commitments."[3] And she insists, "You don't marry races. You marry individuals."[4]

But when she is asked if interracial marriage is only for the strong, she laughs. "*Marriage* is only for the strong. I think it's for people who have a pretty good sense of who they are."[5]

The couple spent their honeymoon on a five-month trip around the world. To help support them on this trip, Peter Edelman gave speeches. The trip allowed Marian Wright Edelman, who loved to travel, time to observe poverty firsthand in Africa, India, Indonesia, and even Vietnam, where American troops were involved in a hopeless war.

Like most of Kennedy's aides, Peter Edelman received a Ford Foundation grant to help him make the transition from legislative assistant to another career. He became the associate director setting up the Robert F. Kennedy Memorial.

Meanwhile Marian's Washington Research Project worked on a report on education in America. She also helped draft a child development bill for Congress that would give more health and education aid to preschoolers. But President Richard Nixon vetoed it. Nixon claimed it would weaken family units, whereas Edelman argued the opposite. She believed it would make poor families stronger by providing better child care for working mothers.

The group tried again, but "by then the right wing had discovered us, and the volume of hate mail scared a lot of people off."[6]

Marian Wright Edelman worked hard to care for the nation's children while producing three of her own. Joshua Robert came along in 1969, Jonah Martin in 1970, and Ezra Benjamin in 1974. As one would expect from a Jewish father and a mother who is a minister's daughter, the boys' first names came from the Bible. Their second names honored people the couple admired who had died: Senator Robert Kennedy, Dr. Martin Luther King, Jr., and Peter Edelman's grandfather, Benjamin Edelman. She has often declared that her children are her proudest achievement.[7]

When Peter Edelman became vice-president of the University of Massachusetts in Boston in 1971, Marian Wright Edelman and their family of (then) two young boys moved with him. She not only became the director of Harvard University's Center for Law and Education there, but she kept in touch with her staff at the Washington Research Project by flying down almost weekly.

In 1971 *Time* magazine gave her one of the first of her many honors: naming her as one of the nation's top 200 young leaders.

Remembering that members of the African-American community watched out for Marian Wright Edelman and the other Wright children when her parents were busy with church business, Marian's mother, Maggie Wright, sent a friend, Miz Amie, from Bennettsville to watch over Marian and Peter's children.

Miz Amie was surrogate grandmother to almost every child on the block, black and white, no matter where the Edelman's lived. She arrived to help with the couple's first child, Joshua, when he was a baby, eventually caring for all three boys. She moved with the Edelmans from Washington to Boston to upstate New York and finally back to Washington. She stayed with the family for thirteen years.

"Miz Amie would sit up on the third floor, and she could look down on everybody's kids," Edelman says. "She never missed a beat about what anyone was doing."[8] Marian Wright Edelman believes:

> There's got to be one consistent adult in a child's life who is always there for them. But children also have to have a whole community. If I know I'm not going to be [home], I always tell the neighbors in the four houses around me. They look out. They're there as surrogate parents. Kids need to know that they're constantly being watched in a supportive way, and that if their parents are not there, they have safe havens they can go to.[9]

Life in a biracial, interfaith household has not been easy. Her sons consider themselves African American. In the foreword to Marian's book, *The Measure of Our Success*, Jonah Edelman talks about the advantages and disadvantages of his life. He refers to himself as a "cultural mulatto, the well-to-do Black liberal wary of the political process, the sheltered Bar-Mitzvah boy who has struggled with his blackness. . . ."[10]

As each boy turned thirteen, they had a Baptist bar mitzvah out in the backyard, presided over by both a rabbi and a Baptist minister. This ceremony, created by the Edelman family, went along with the family goal of raising the children with fundamental values and respect for the religious and racial heritage of both parents. She says, "I am less concerned about whether my kids grow up Jewish or Christian than if they have inner strength and a sense of service."[11]

She is aware that they had a struggle growing up with a foot in each world:

> Sure, they struggle. It's very difficult for any young people to figure out who they are. My children just have an extra couple of struggles. But it is out of struggle that you grow. If things are too easy, life is a whole lot less interesting.[12]

Jonah Edelman remembers the love that lies at the core of his family life, the love that gave him strength. He says, "My parents raised me to be an individual, letting me make my own mistakes and supporting me when I did."[13] Marian and Peter Edelman praised their children with the words, "We are VERY proud of you," always with the emphasis on the word *very*. Jonah says that phrase always "boosted me immeasurably through the years. It still does."[14]

Marian Wright Edelman told the world how well her children turned out, despite her being a working mother, in her book, *The Measure of Our Success*. She wrote, "I am so proud of each of you [children] in every way, and thank you for making your parents look terrific. . . ."[15]

Juggling work and family is hard for every working mother. Edelman declares she was, at times, "hanging on by my fingernails. It was mild insanity."[16]

But she had it somewhat easier than most working mothers. Because she always was the boss, she gave herself the option of choosing family over work. If a child was sick and their father could not stay with them, she could leave her office or skip a meeting to care for them. She could even hold her staff meetings at her own home, staying within earshot of the sick children.

One time she turned down an invitation to speak at a Democratic National Convention because she had promised Ezra that she would take him to the All-Star baseball game. Her friends were shocked. But she stood firm. She insisted that there were many fine speakers able to speak at the convention but not that many things a mom can do with a teenage boy.

Still, she does regret all the sports games she was late for or missed. But she was so proud of her children the day that Ezra got hit by a baseball and had to be rushed to the emergency room. His older brother, Joshua, swept him up, transported him to the hospital, then calmly informed his parents.

In Marian Wright Edelman's book she lists many typical working mother's regrets and asks her children's forgiveness for:

> all the times I talked when I should have listened;
> got angry when I should have been patient;
> acted when I should have waited;
> feared when I should have delighted;
> scolded when I should have encouraged;
> criticized when I should have complimented;
> said no when I should have said yes and yes when I should have said no.[17]

And yet her children say they never thought of her as an absent mother figure. She did make it to many of their sports games. In addition, they knew they could call her anytime at work and she would always be happy to hear from them.

She wanted to make sure her own children had all their physical needs met and lots of love. But she also believed that as a parent she could not ignore the other children around the country who might not have the advantages her own sons had.

Peter and Marian Wright Edelman are proud of their children. Shown here is Jonah Edelman's graduation from Yale University in 1992. From left to right: Marian, Ezra, Jonah, Peter, and Joshua.

The weekly flights down to Washington, D.C., from Boston and New York had to have been exhausting for her, but it did not slow this energetic mom down. Instead of closing down the Washington Research Project, she decided to expand it. Thus the Children's Defense Fund was born.

8

The Children's Defense Fund

By 1973, Marian Wright Edelman discovered that "The country was tired of the concerns of the sixties. When you talked about poor people or black people, you faced a shrinking audience."[1] However, remembering the effect that starving child had on Robert Kennedy, "I got the idea that children might be a very effective way to broaden the base for change."[2]

Therefore she established the Children's Defense Fund (CDF) in 1973 to provide a voice for a group of people fifty million strong who had no political power in the United States—children. After all, children cannot vote. Children have no voice in government. And yet so many of the laws that passed affect them.

Looking back on her work as a private civil rights lawyer in Mississippi, she realized she had learned that she could only have a limited, though important, impact on meeting the needs of a few poor families with children:

> I also learned that critical civil and political rights would not mean much to a hungry, homeless, illiterate child and family if they lacked the social and economic means to exercise them. And so children—my own and other people's—became the passion of my personal and professional life.[3]

The CDF was created as a nonprofit organization that is loyal to no political party. It works to give a better life for poor children of all races and classes. Its mission is to educate the nation about the needs of children and encourage preventive investment in children before they get sick, drop out of school, suffer family breakdown or too-early pregnancy, or get into trouble.

"We do not have a child to waste," Edelman declares again and again. "We will not be a strong country unless we invest in every one of our children. . . . All children are essential to America's future."[4]

At first, the CDF was financed by private foundation grants. Gradually their budget was expanded by donations from businesses and private individuals. Some of the first projects they investigated included the reasons so many of the nation's school-aged children were not enrolled in school, the treatment of institutionalized children, juvenile justice, and the use of children in medical experiments.

Edelman fully believes in the old saying, "Knowledge is power." Her staff works hard researching and identifying problems that affect America's children. The reports they issue are not just dry statistics. In addition to itemizing the problems, these reports propose possible solutions. But CDF does not stop with just issuing reports. Edelman and her staff then walk the halls of the Capitol trying to convince the legislators in Congress to either enact new laws or to enforce the laws that are already on the books. This activity is called lobbying.

Many representatives of groups in the United States meet with the members of Congress in Washington to discuss laws and bills under consideration. These people are called lobbyists. Every lobbyist tries to convince legislators to enact or support laws favorable to the cause they represent. The CDF has been an official lobbyist group in Congress ever since it was formed.

Edelman contends, "Our problem is not one of law but of making laws work, getting them funded, riding the bureaucrats and enabling people to take advantage of what Congress intended."[5]

Her passionate push for the rights of children has made her nationally known as "the children's crusader."[6]

Under the conservative Republican presidencies of Richard Nixon and Gerald Ford in the late 1960s and 1970s, very little money was spent for social services. The CDF grew more hopeful when liberal Democrat

WHEN IT'S BUDGET CUTTING TIME, THEY ALWAYS START WITH THE EASIEST TARGETS.

The CDF believes that child welfare is one of the first programs eliminated by the government during budget cutting time.

Jimmy Carter was elected in 1976. But he also turned out to be conservative about spending money.

However, the CDF worked to increase the federal food program for the poor and to expand the Head Start program and Medicaid coverage for children. Their efforts paid off with a gradual doubling of funding.

When Peter Edelman was offered a teaching position at Georgetown University Law Center in 1979, the whole family moved back to the Washington, D.C., area. Now that she no longer was limited to the weekly flying visits, Marian Wright Edelman could concentrate on lobbying Congress. She and her CDF staff helped herd a child-welfare bill through Congress in 1980.

The CDF not only takes the results of its research to Congress, but it assists Congress with the drafting of legislation, provides testimony before the lawmakers, and monitors federal agencies to see that they carry out the intent as well as the letter of the law. It also brings its findings to the attention of the public, educating them in the needs of children everywhere. It works with individuals and groups to change policies and practices resulting in neglect or mistreatment of millions of children and advocates a strong parental and community role in decision-making.

Some lobbyists in Washington, D.C., use money to influence Congress; Edelman influences them with cold hard facts and her ability to talk faster than most people. There were no lobbyists in the Capitol of the United

States to speak up for children until she created the CDF.

Her influence on Congress is so strong that Senator Edward Kennedy of Massachusetts has called her "the 101st Senator" for children's issues on Capitol Hill.[7]

Edelman could attack as well as persuade. While another child-welfare bill was being discussed in Congress in the 1970s, she leveled an attack on President Carter himself. She wrote:

> If the drastic cuts which your administration is now considering to children's programs occur, it will establish once and for all the hypocrisy of your professed concern about children and families in America.[8]

Her lobbying skills have become legendary. One senator admitted that he knew dozens of male senators who tremble and try to hide in the men's room when they hear she is prowling the Senate Office Building. She is aware of her reputation. She often compares herself to the nineteenth-century civil rights pioneer Sojourner Truth, who traveled the United States as an antislavery and woman's rights speaker. During one of Sojourner Truth's speeches, a heckler yelled out that he cared no more for her anti-slavery talk "than for a flea bite." "Maybe not," Truth replied, "but the Lord willing, I'll keep you scratching."[9]

When asked about her lobbying skills, Edelman admits, "There's no great magic about it. You just have

The Children's Defense Fund, located in Washington, D.C., is housed in this building just a few blocks from the Capitol building.

to stay on people and make it easier for them to do what you want them to do than not to do it. I'm a good pest is what I am."[10]

She is aware that people view her differently than they do the usual male lobbyists. When the House Ways and Means Committee accused her of trying to bully members of Congress, she explained, but made no excuses for her actions, "I'm very conscious of the disparity between the way people view women and men." They expect "women to act differently, not play hardball with men."[11] And when it comes to children, Edelman plays hardball with the best of them. Her husband, Peter Edelman, says:

> She has an absolutely superb strategic and tactical sense. . . . She understands how the system works. She's as tough and determined as anyone can be, but always within the rules of the system.[12]

A tribute to her skill is the fact that at times she has been able to enlist both the liberal Senator Edward Kennedy and the conservative Senator Orrin Hatch onto the same side—hers. She feels all sides should work together for the common cause of children everywhere.

When Ronald Reagan was elected president in 1980, she discovered that the battle is never over. One of the first things President Reagan wanted to do when he took office in 1981, after the biggest landslide victory ever, was repeal the child-welfare act. But the CDF and their friends in Congress managed to block that move as well as some of the other moves by the Republicans to disband or weaken Head Start and the WIC (Women, Infants, and Children) nutrition program.

During the 1980s, Edelman and her staff appeared to be the one lonely voice speaking out for government funding for the poor as the Reagan administration attempted to tear apart the welfare system so carefully built by the Democrats over the years. But she says, "I'm proudest that things didn't get as bad as they could have. We kept the erosion from being worse."[13]

The CDF continually sends their reports and statistics to Capitol Hill. Their annual report, now called *The State of America's Children Yearbook*, has become almost required reading for every member of Congress.

In 1983, Edelman noticed from the CDF statistics that 55.5 percent of all African-American babies were born out of wedlock, many of them to teenage girls. It just hit her over the head—that situation insured African-American child poverty for the next generation. She decided something must be done to stop this, or at least slow it down.

And so the CDF launched its national campaign to provide positive life options for youth, including prevention of teen pregnancy. The still-ongoing multimedia campaign tries to reach teens wherever they gather with advertisements on buses, trains, and subways; eye-catching posters in schools, libraries, subway stations,

The one on the left will finish high school before the one on the right.

As part of its mission, the CDF works to help prevent teen pregnancy.

and bus stops of teens of all races experiencing the results of unplanned pregnancy; and television and radio public service announcements.

All these spots have succeeded in pointing out the dangers without preaching, realizing that nothing is less effective than preaching to the young people who desperately need the information.

The other half of the campaign, which provides positive life options, has a simple purpose—to keep teens in school so they can be successful later in life. It provides activities that build self-confidence and improves the work-related skills necessary to find decent jobs when they graduate.

Each year the CDF honors a few teenagers who beat the odds by excelling in school despite the hardships in their lives.

In addition, the CDF organized a national prenatal care campaign, which included education about birth control, and an Adolescent Pregnancy Prevention Clearinghouse, which offered help (both information and technical assistance) to local prevention programs around the country.

Edelman and the CDF admit that the intensive education and employment training that teens need, both before and after childbearing, could cost the same or perhaps more than welfare does. But it would mean trying to change cultural signals, to change the way people think—and that does not happen overnight. Just thinking about the cost might depress some people. But not Edelman. She warns that the cycle of poverty and pregnancy cannot be broken quickly or cheaply. She just considers it another step in her fight to pull children out of poverty.

In 1984 Edelman suddenly realized what it felt like to be orphaned when her mother died. It surprised her that at age forty-five she would feel this way. Her mother had continued with her community and church work in Bennettsville until a few weeks before her death. It often makes Edelman feel sad that she cannot just pick up the phone and ask her mother for advice anymore.[14]

In 1985 Edelman organized and presided over the CDF's first Pregnancy Prevention Conference.

She also runs the annual national conference of the Children's Defense Fund. These yearly meetings draw over 2,500 religious leaders and social and health workers in addition to community organizers who work with children and families.

Edelman's sister, Olive Wright Covington, says, "The people who come to these conventions are the 'doers', the 'worker bees.'"[15] They attend as many workshops as possible and then take the information back to their workplace and spread the word.

The three-day conference offers over one hundred different workshops. Some of the workshops inform children's advocates about successful programs throughout the United States with tips on beginning

DEVELOP YOUR BODY AND YOU COULD BE A FOOTBALL PLAYER.

DEVELOP YOUR MIND AND YOU COULD OWN THE TEAM.

This poster is an example of the CDF's national campaign to provide positive life options for youth. Keeping teens in school is an important theme of the CDF.

such programs. Others are how-to sessions or "train the trainer" sessions. With these training sessions, the CDF staff and other hired speakers offer training in such things as how to grow phone and letter trees, how to resolve conflicts, how to handle broadcast media, how to have a better relationship with your bank, how to do better fundraising, how to use violence data, and how to influence your legislators in Congress and the state government.

Most of the people attending the conference carry away the same feeling as Lisa Shulock, an advocate from Philadelphia who works with the Citizens for Children and Youth, did. "It's a wonderful networking opportunity. It invigorates me and gives me lots of ideas and I can go back to work with new energy."[16]

9

A Voice for Children

Although the general view of some of the American public appears to be that poverty and welfare mothers are largely African American, Edelman is out to prove that perception wrong. She constantly quotes facts and figures proving that a good number of poor children are white, not black or brown, living in rural and suburban areas, not only in the inner cities. However, she does not deny the existence of patches of poverty in the African-American areas of inner cities.

She appeals to the African-American community to join her in focusing on economic and social issues—including those patches of poverty. She urges every African American to find a way "to be there for our kids. . . . If every Black church placed one Black foster child in one Black family," she suggests, "we'd have no more [black] children in foster care."[1]

By 1987, Edelman's efforts at lobbying had paid off in increases in nine federal programs known as the Children's Initiative, including an increase in Medicaid coverage for expectant mothers and their children. This helped counteract the effects of the ten million dollar cuts in social services enacted by the Reagan Administration.

During the presidential election campaign of 1988, Edelman saw hopeful signs that the fiscal tightness of the United States government toward programs to help children might loosen up. Both of the presidential contenders, Vice President George Bush and Governor Michael Dukakis of Massachusetts, claimed an interest in the growing need for day care for children of working mothers.

The CDF's efforts to publicize the plight of children was resulting in more reports in newspapers and magazines about child abuse and neglect, poverty, and hunger.

Edelman decided it was time to try to push for another comprehensive child-care bill. She called it the ABC Bill, a catchy name for the Act for Better Child Care. It was the culmination of over a year of research, based on input from over 170 people and organizations. By the time it was written, the CDF staff thought it included most of what was most urgently needed by

Marian Wright Edelman appeals to the African-American community to join her in focusing on economic and social issues, including poverty.

America's children. Among its objectives was a request for $2.5 billion (for the first year's expenses) for programs enforcing the highest standards of quality, health, and safety for child care. The law would help families with low and moderate incomes pay for this child care.

The CDF submitted it to the House of Representatives in August of 1988. With the help of two supporters, Representative Tom Downey of New York and Representative George Miller of California, the House of Representatives passed the bill and sent it on to the Senate.

However, Senator Orrin Hatch of Utah had introduced a similar bill, called the Hatch Bill, in the Senate at the same time that also called for child care reform but did not offer as much money or as many services as the ABC Bill. It also would allow the state government to control the monies. From Edelman's fight with the Mississippi government over Head Start funds, she knew that she could not trust state governments to act in the best interests of children.

The ABC Bill stalled in the Senate and then died. Several other compromise bills were proposed in Congress. But none of them included the broad sweep of services and money of the ABC Bill. Then in November of 1989, Representatives Downey and Miller abandoned the ABC Bill and decided to support one of the other bills in hopes of getting something on child care passed.

A compromise child-care bill was finally passed in 1990 supplying only $600 million.[2] CDF supporter Amy Wilkins told a reporter from *Nations* magazine that it seemed that somehow child care was not as important to the politicians on Capitol Hill as the Persian Gulf War or the economic disaster centering around the failure of many savings and loan banks in the late 1980s.[3] Still, it was a victory of sorts. It was the first major national child-care bill that had been passed for many years.

"Marian is the best advocate I've ever met," Senator Jay Rockefeller of West Virginia, one of Marian's staunchest allies in Congress, once said. "The Children's Defense Fund has provided all of the intensity and heat behind children's issues."[4]

In January of 1992, she won an additional $200 million from the Bush administration to help fund the national Head Start's educational program.

Another side of Marian Wright Edelman was seen in 1992 as well. A slim book of warm humor and motherly advice aimed at her sons but published for the world to share on Mother's Day suddenly hit the bestseller lists. *The Measure of Our Success: A Letter to My Children and Yours* was not Edelman's first book. She had written speeches, statistical reports, and pamphlets for the CDF for years. An earlier book, *Families in Peril: An Agenda for Social Change*, based on the series of lectures she had delivered at Harvard in 1986, had been published by

This flag clearly states the goal of the CDF, "Leave No Child Behind."

Harvard Press but did not catch the public's eye and heart like *Measure of Our Success* did.

This slim book caught on by word-of-mouth. By the end of 1992, there were 200,000 copies in print, and it had spent sixteen weeks on *The New York Times* bestseller list. It is still selling strong in paperback.

The book came about through a combination of factors. First, several years earlier Edelman was looking for something she could give her oldest son on his twenty-first birthday. It came to her that she thought she had never vocalized the values she had learned from her parents that have driven her all her life. So she wrote a letter to him.

At the same time, her soon-to-be editor at Beacon Press had gathered together a selection of Edelman's writings and sent them to Edelman with the suggestion she think about forming a book out of them. The combination of the two projects meshed into what became *The Measure of Our Success*.

Along with the letter to her sons, in this book she presents a carefully thought-out list of "Twenty-Five Lessons for Life:"

> **Lesson 1:** There is no free lunch. Don't feel entitled to anything you don't sweat and struggle for.
>
> **Lesson 2:** Set goals and work quietly and systematically toward them.
>
> **Lesson 3:** Assign yourself. Don't wait around to be told what to do.

Lesson 4: Never work just for money or for power. They won't save your soul or build a decent family or help you sleep at night.

Lesson 5: Don't be afraid of taking risks or of being criticized.

Lesson 6: Take parenting and family life seriously and insist that those you work for and who represent you do.

Lesson 7: Remember that your wife is not your mother or your maid, but your partner and friend.

Lesson 8: Forming families is serious business.

Lesson 9: Be honest.

Lesson 10: Remember and help America remember that the fellowship of human beings is more important than the fellowship of race and class and gender in a democratic society.

Lesson 11: Sell the shadow for the substance. [Struggle to keep personal, organizational, and public priorities straight.]

Lesson 12: Never give up.

Lesson 13: Be confident that you can make a difference.

Lesson 14: Don't ever stop learning and improving your mind.

Lesson 15: Don't be afraid of hard work or of teaching your children to work.

Lesson 16: "Slow Down and Live." A job done too . . . hurriedly is never well done.

Lesson 17: Choose your friends carefully.

Lesson 18: Be a can-do, will-try person.

Lesson 19: Try to live in the present.

Lesson 20: Use your political and economic power for the community and others less fortunate.

Lesson 21: Listen for "the sound of the genuine" within yourself and others.

Lesson 22: You are in charge of your own attitude.

Lesson 23: Remember your roots, your history, and the forebears' shoulders on which you stand.

Lesson 24: Be reliable. Be faithful. Finish what you start.

Lesson 25: Always remember that you are never alone.[5]

The other major change in her life in 1992 involved her good friend, the chair of the CDF's board of directors, Hillary Rodham Clinton.

In 1969 Hillary Rodham, an intelligent and ambitious young woman, heard Edelman speak at Yale University where Rodham was studying law. With her usual graceful cool, Edelman lectured gently but forcefully on the needs of underprivileged children.

Afterwards Rodham pushed her way through the crowds surrounding Marian Wright Edelman, determined to tell her how her speech had moved her. Rodham describes their meeting this way:

> I went up to her after she finished speaking and said, 'I want to work for you this summer.' She [Edelman] said, 'I have no paying jobs [at the

Washington Research Project].' I said, '. . . If I can find out how to be paid, would you put me to work?' She [Edelman] said, 'Why should I refuse an offer like that?'[6]

Rodham began work as a summer volunteer, participating in the research project to find out why two million U.S. children were not in school. The report concluded that many public schools were excluding children who either did not speak English or were too poor to pay for books or needed medical help. The end result of this activity was a federal law guaranteeing education for disabled children.

When she graduated from law school, Rodham became a staff lawyer for the group. "The world opened up to me," Rodham Clinton explains, "and gave me a vision of what it ought to be because of the work of people like Marian."[7]

During their many years of working together, Rodham Clinton and Edelman became close friends, even to the point of Rodham Clinton choosing the Sidwell Friends School for her daughter Chelsea when the Clintons moved into the White House. The school was the one to which the Edelmans had sent their sons.

Hillary Rodham Clinton became chair of the CDF board in 1986 and served until 1992, when she resigned to help her husband, Bill Clinton, run for the presidency. The next chair, Donna Shalala, Chancellor of the University of Wisconsin at Madison and a member of the board since 1980, retired within a year when she was appointed to serve in President Clinton's cabinet as secretary of Health and Human Services. (Peter Edelman serves as Shalala's counselor as well as continuing to be a professor of law at Georgetown University.)

After Bill Clinton's election in 1992, rumor had him appointing Edelman to various governmental offices—even Supreme Court Justice. But Edelman denied the rumors. She would rather be the wasp buzzing around, outside, occasionally stinging the government in the right places to implement services for children. And as for the post of Supreme Court Justice? Edelman says: "I can't think of anything I'd like less to do than that. That's not where my talents . . . [or] interests lie. That's not who I am. I'd be bored to tears."[8]

"She is doing what the Lord put her on earth to do, be a voice for children," CDF spokesperson Stella Ogata explains.[9]

10

"Service Is the Rent You Pay for Living"

Edelman's goal for the 1990s is to eliminate juvenile poverty by the year 2000. To ensure this, her campaign has become four-pronged. Under the umbrella heading of "Leave No Child Behind," she and the CDF advocate:

1) *A Head Start* for every child—Good preschool, child care, and Head Start programs to help children get ready for school, keep up in school, and prepare for the future.

2) *A Healthy Start* for every child—Comprehensive health care for every child and pregnant woman, starting with prenatal care and including immunizations and preventive care.

3) *A Fair Start* for every child—Jobs for parents at decent wages, child support enforcement, refundable tax credits for families with children, and help to keep family problems from turning into crises.

4) *A Safe Start* for every child—After-school and other preventive programs to keep children safe and challenged, plus regulation of nonsporting firearms and ammunition as dangerous products.[1]

The main thrust of these goals is prevention. She sells these goals to businesses and community leaders by emphasizing that an ounce of prevention now will create productive citizens (workers) when they grow up.

One way she has developed support for her projects among the business world is by a program called Child Watch Visitation. The program's thesis is very simple. It is based upon that incident in Mississippi when Edelman took the senators into the homes of poor people in the poverty-stricken Delta area, allowing them to see firsthand what these people faced every day.

Child Watch Visitation simply adds the faces and stories of real children to the statistics and reports. It is easy to tune out lists of numbers. But it is much harder to forget the face of someone you have actually met and whose story you have heard. That sticks with you.

By 1994, the Child Watch Visitation had been used in over seventy-five cities, proving its effectiveness each time. The procedure is simple. Volunteer organizations, with help from CDF, locate the situation and set up the visit. However, since few people willingly take time off from work to see someone whose life has had a miserable outcome, an influential person in the community is chosen to invite the other business leaders, clergy, and legislators.

For example, first the group is taken to see the one-pound premature babies, small enough to hold in the palm of your hand, lying in their incubators connected to tubes that supply their basic needs, struggling to keep alive. Then, on the return trip by bus, the Child Watch organizer gives the group reports and statistics proving that had the mothers of those babies received $1,000 of prenatal care, it would have prevented the $2,000-a-day expense of keeping those babies alive.

But Child Watch does not stop there. As with all CDF organized efforts, the tour guide goes on to tell the group *how* they can become effective child advocates and help solve these problems themselves.

Businesspeople can understand the dollars and cents reasoning that healthy children reaching school age ready to learn will grow up to be productive workers. Likewise, they understand their workers will have increased productivity when their children are provided for. It just makes good business sense.

Catholic Archbishop John Roach of Minneapolis, Minnesota, participated in a Child Watch Visitation program there. Afterwards, he declared, "Earlier . . . someone called us the movers and shakers of the religious community. After this experience, we are the moved and the shaken."[2]

Sometimes the participants come up with solutions themselves. One distinguished woman who visited the boarder-baby ward at Washington, D.C., General

Hospital, realized that there was no place for these children to play. She proposed to raise money for a play area for them.

Edelman has been accused of trying to solve 1990s problems with old-fashioned, 1960s liberal solutions. Her detractors contend that government money does not solve social problems. She responds: "People ought to be able to distinguish between throwing money at problems and investing in success."[3] She believes in the latter.

Corporations large and small have responded to the appeals made by Edelman to support the CDF and its work. Most of the almost $11 million budget supporting the over 120 employees of the CDF and their activities are supplied by corporations like Chrysler, Coca-Cola, and Morgan Guaranty Trust.

Other companies, such as the department store Bloomingdale's, have helped by placing the CDF's toll-free telephone number on their store shopping bags. Some companies such as Ben & Jerry's, Vermont's Finest Ice Cream & Frozen Yogurt, have placed the number right on their products—the backs of Ben & Jerry's Peace Pops and the lids of their SMOOTH ice cream. The CDF is careful about controlling the messages on Ben & Jerry's items. Their partnership in public education about the needs of children has grown with leaps and bounds since 1992 when Ben & Jerry's employees voted to support a cause that helps children.

The recording at the other end of the toll-free number asks the caller to leave his or her name and address. The CDF will send the caller a kit telling how to contact Congress. The kit includes updates on children's issues and tells what one can do in one's own community. By 1994, 22,000 names had been collected this way.

Edelman insists, "If we don't begin to support families and put kids first, the country's going to go down the drain. People always say to me: 'We admire your work. Keep it up.' All I want to say is: 'Help! Help!'" [4]

It is this kind of help from the business community that keeps Edelman optimistic about the possibility of success in her lifetime.

Edelman is the spearhead for all of the CDF's activity. She gives speeches and lectures, sometimes fifty a year. She often works twelve-hour days, keeping her energy up by nibbling on apples. She writes reports and articles for newspapers and magazines. She visits potential Child Visitation sites. She testifies at government hearings. Into all these projects, she pours her passion and her sense of urgency, bringing statistics to life. She commands everyone who listens to her to pay attention, to feel the pain she feels, and to do something about it.

If a reporter forgets to bring a tape recorder along to a Marian Wright Edelman interview, he or she will be overwhelmed by the speed and intensity of her words.

When Marian Wright Edelman visited the Ben & Jerry's factory to cement the relationship between the CDF and Ben & Jerry's, she spent some time working on the assembly line.

That reporter will not be able to keep up, even with shorthand. At the drop of a hat, Edelman will expound on any subject, turning it to her favorite concern—children and their needs—emphasizing points with her hand or the pounding of a fist on the podium or table. Her soft, southern voice rolls over the listener until he or she is convinced of the pure logic of her argument.

Lynn Bowersox-Megginson, the CDF director of media relations says, "Marian is a master at making statistics live with clever analogies and comparisons."[5] *Rolling Stone* magazine once called her "America's mom."[6] *Psychology Today* agrees, calling her "the nation's top mom."[7] This mom looks out for America's children by pushing the government and local groups to act in the best interest of children.

But she is also her children's mom. The Edelman boys are grown now and live on their own. Edelman said in 1992:

> We're having a terrible empty-nest trauma at the moment. One side of me can't stop crying. But the other side realizes, my goodness, Peter and I can go away together for the weekend. We don't *have* to be here. . . . It's very nice to begin to know your children as adults.[8]

Judith Viorst, author of a *Redbook* magazine interview with Marian Wright Edelman in 1993, agrees. She says:

> Their sons are now impressive adults in their own right. Joshua . . . [is] a Harvard graduate who teaches geography and medieval history . . . Jonah

[is] a Yale graduate and a Rhodes Scholar . . .
studying . . . at Oxford. And Ezra . . . [is] at Yale
. . . interested in sports journalism.[9]

Marian and Peter Edelman still live in their comfortable old stucco house in the Cleveland Park section of Washington, D.C., surrounded by books and plants and some treasured things from her childhood home in Bennettsville. The piano in the corner is her refuge in times of stress and her way of expressing times of joy. Music is still an important part of her life. It is her "psychiatrist,"[10] she told an interviewer. When members of her family visit with their instruments, the walls reverberate with song.

Edelman enjoys reading for pleasure, often squeezing time for it in the bathtub. And she wishes she had more time to indulge in her passion for painting. Another form of relaxation is her garden. Being a city garden, it is not large, but she can go way down into the old oak trees at the lower end of it where no telephone can bother her. Often in the early morning, she will retreat to a little meditation hut there. Her sister, Olive Wright Covington, explains:

> Or, when she feels the need for completely recharging her energies, she'll go to a convent for silent time— reading and meditating. That's where she gets inspiration and vision. When you spend a lot of time with a lot of people, you need time to recharge your batteries. She does this several times a year.[11]

As you would expect from the daughter and granddaughter of Baptist ministers, the life of the church and prayer is second nature to her.

Marian Wright Edelman's childhood home is now used as an outpost for the CDF. Her sister, Olive Wright Covington, runs the operations there.

Robert Coles, one of her oldest supporters, explains Edelman this way:

> I don't think anyone has done as much for America's children as she has in the last 25 years. There's a moral energy she brings to this work that goes back to her childhood. There is always in Marian the minister's daughter from South Carolina.[12]

Edelman agrees:

> When my mother died, an old white man in my hometown of Bennettsville asked me what I do. In a flash I realized that in my work at the Children's Defense Fund I do exactly what my parents did—just on a different scale.[13]

For the rest of her life, Edelman will continue to live her life according to the code she learned as a child—"service is the rent you pay for living, not something you do in your spare time."[14]

Chronology

1939—Born in Bennettsville, South Carolina, on June 6.

1954—Arthur Jerome Wright (her father) dies.

1956—Graduates from Marlboro Training School and enters Spelman College.

1958—Spends summer at the Sorbonne in Paris, France; spends academic year at the University of Geneva in Switzerland.

1959—Spends summer in Russia.

1960—Participates in the Atlanta Sit-In and is arrested; graduates as class valedictorian from Spelman and enters Yale Law School.

1963—Receives her law degree.

1964—Goes to Jackson, Mississippi, as director of the NAACP Legal Defense and Education Fund office.

1967—Takes Senators Robert Kennedy and Joseph Clark on a tour of the Mississippi Delta area; introduced to Peter Benjamin Edelman.

1968—Moves to Washington, D.C.; starts the Washington Research Project; Martin Luther King, Jr., is assassinated in April; Robert F. Kennedy is assassinated in June; marries Peter Edelman on July 14.

1971—*Time* magazine names her "One of America's Top 200 Young Leaders"; is the first African-American woman elected to the Yale University Corporation (1971–1977).

1973—Founds the Children's Defense Fund.

1979—The Edelman family moves back to Washington, D.C., area.

1980—National Women's Political Caucus honors her with their Leadership Award; is the first African-American and second woman to chair the board of Spelman College (1980–1987.)

1984—Maggie Leola Bowen Wright (her mother) dies.

1987—*Families in Peril: An Agenda for Social Change* is published.

1990—Lobbies for and gets Congress to pass a child-welfare bill.

1992—Hillary Rodham Clinton retires as chair of CDF board in order to help her husband run for the presidency of the United States; for the first time, the CDF (and Marian Wright Edelman) has friends in the White House; *The Measure of Our Success: A Letter to My Children and Yours* is published.

1993—Is awarded Outstanding Mother Award by the National Mother's Day committee and the Lawyer of the Year award by the Washington, D.C., bar association.

1993 -1996—Is on the United States Olympic Committee for the Summer Games held in Atlanta, Georgia, in 1996.

1994—*Ebony* magazine names her one of the year's Most Influential Black Americans; *Parenting* magazine awards her the Parenting Lifetime Achievement Award.

For Further Information

For further information about Marian Wright Edelman and the Children's Defense Fund, write:

Children's Defense Fund
25 E Street, NW
Washington, D.C. 20001

Chapter Notes

Chapter 1

1. Clara Bingham, "Saint Marian," *Harper's Bazaar,* February 1993, p. 157.

2. Wallace Terry, "We Don't Have a Child to Waste, an Interview with Marian Wright Edelman," *Parade,* February 14, 1993, p. 5.

3. Julie Beyer, interview with the author, CDF National Convention, Cincinnati, Ohio, March 1994.

4. Terry, p. 5.

Chapter 2

1. Marian Wright Edelman, *The Measure of Our Success: A Letter to My Children and Yours* (Boston: Beacon Press, 1992), p. 3.

2. Olive Wright Covington, interview with the author, February 3, 1994.

3. Ibid.

4. Marian Wright Edelman, "On This Mother's Day, a Message," *Parade,* May 8, 1994, p. 5.

5. Covington interview.

6. Judith Viorst, "The Woman Behind the First Lady (Children's Advocate Marian Wright Edelman Influences Hillary Clinton)," *Redbook,* June 1993, p. 66.

7. Norman Atkins, "Marian Wright Edelman: On the Front Lines of the Battle to Save America's Children," *Rolling Stone*, December 10, 1992, p. 202.

8. Covington interview.

9. Edelman, *The Measure of Our Success*, p. 49.

10. Ibid., p. 4.

11. Beverly Guy-Sheffall, "Marian Wright Edelman," *Notable Black American Women* (Detroit: Gale Research, 1992), p. 309.

12. Edelman, *The Measure of Our Success*, p. 39.

13. Covington interview.

14. Wallace Terry, "We Don't Have a Child to Waste, an Interview with Marian Wright Edelman," *Parade*, February 14, 1993, p. 4.

15. Covington interview.

16. Edelman, *The Measure of Our Success*, p. 5.

17. Terry, p. 4.

Chapter 3

1. Wallace Terry, "We Don't Have a Child to Waste, an Interview with Marian Wright Edelman," *Parade*, February 14, 1993, p. 4.

2. Ibid.

3. Ibid, p. 5.

4. Judith Graham, ed., "Edelman, Marian Wright," *Current Biography Yearbook, 1992* (New York: H. W. Wilson, 1992), p. 179.

5. Frank B. Lantham, *The Rise and Fall of "Jim Crow," 1865–1964; the Negro's Struggle to Win the "Equal Protection of the Laws"* (New York: Franklin Watts, 1969), p. 8.

6. Stuart Kallen, *The Civil Rights Movement* (Edina, Minn.: Abdo and Daughters, 1990), p. 14.

7. Latham, p. 7

8. Ibid, p. 29.

9. "Mother Marian," *Psychology Today*, July–August 1993, p. 30.

10. Marian Wright Edelman, *The Measure of Our Success: A Letter to My Children and Yours* (Boston: Beacon Press, 1992), p. 3.

11. Graham, p. 179.

12. "They Cannot Fend for Themselves," *Time*, March 23, 1987, p. 27.

13. Ibid.

14. Terry, p. 4.

15. Edelman, p. 7.

16. Latham, p. 68.

Chapter 4

1. Marian Wright Edelman, "On This Mother's Day, a Message," *Parade*, May 8, 1994, p. 5.

2. Olive Wright Covington, interview with the author, February 3, 1994.

3. Ibid.

4. Beverly Guy-Sheffall, "Marian Wright Edelman," *Notable Black American Women* (Detroit: Gale Research, 1992), p. 310.

5. Covington interview.

6. Ibid.

7. Guy-Sheffall, p. 310.

8. Judith Graham, ed., "Edelman, Marian Wright," *Current Biography Yearbook, 1992* (New York: H. W. Wilson, 1992), p. 179–180.

9. Guy-Sheffall, p. 310.

10. Ellen Levine, *If You Lived at the Time of Martin Luther King* (New York: Scholastic, 1990), p. 32.

11. Steve Otfinoski, *Marian Wright Edelman: Outspoken Defender of Children's Rights* (Woodbridge, Conn.: Blackbirch Press, 1991), p. 14.

12. Ibid.

13. Graham, p. 180.

14. Otfinoski, p. 15.

15. Wallace Terry, "We Don't Have a Child to Waste, an Interview with Marian Wright Edelman," *Parade*, February 14, 1993, p. 5.

16. Covington interview.

17. Terry, p. 5.

Chapter 5

1. Olive Wright Covington, interview with the author, February 3, 1994.

2. Wallace Terry, "We Don't Have a Child to Waste, an Interview with Marian Wright Edelman," *Parade*, February 14, 1993, p. 5.

3. Frank B. Lantham, *The Rise and Fall of "Jim Crow," 1865–1964; the Negro's Struggle to Win the "Equal Protection of the Laws"* (New York: Franklin Watts, 1969), p. 58.

4. C. Vann Woodward, *The Strange Career of Jim Crow* (New York: Oxford University Press, 1974), p. 170.

5. Steve Otfinoski, *Marian Wright Edelman: Outspoken Defender of Children's Rights* (Woodbridge, Conn.: Blackbirch Press, 1991), p. 18.

6. Terry, p. 5.

7. Otfinoski, p. 19.

8. Ellen Levine, *If You Lived at the Time of Martin Luther King* (New York: Scholastic, 1990), p. 59.

9. Judith Graham, ed., "Edelman, Marian Wright," *Current Biography Yearbook, 1992* (New York: H. W. Wilson, 1992), p. 180.

10. Marian Wright Edelman, "On This Mother's Day, a Message," *Parade*, May 8, 1994, p. 6.

11. Covington interview.

Chapter 6

1. C. Vann Woodward, *The Strange Career of Jim Crow* (New York: Oxford University Press, 1974), p. 184.

2. Milton Meltzer, ed., *The Black Americans: A History in Their Own Words, 1619–1983* (New York: Thomas Y. Crowell, 1984), p. 265.

3. Woodward, p. 184.

4. Judith Viorst, "The Woman Behind the First Lady (Children's Advocate Marian Wright Edelman Influences Hillary Clinton)," *Redbook*, June 1993, p. 66.

5. Steve Otfinoski, *Marian Wright Edelman: Outspoken Defender of Children's Rights* (Woodbridge, Conn.: Blackbirch Press, 1991), p. 21.

6. Wallace Terry, "We Don't Have a Child to Waste, an Interview with Marian Wright Edelman," *Parade*, February 14, 1993, p. 5.

7. Beverly Guy-Sheffall, "Marian Wright Edelman," *Notable Black American Women* (Detroit: Gale Research, 1992), p. 310.

8. Norman Atkins, "Marian Wright Edelman: On the Front Lines of the Battle to Save America's Children," *Rolling Stone*, December 10, 1992, p. 130.

9. Otfinoski, p. 22.

10. Ibid, p. 25.

11. Matthew S. Scott, "The Great Defender," *Black Enterprise*, May 1992, p. 67.

12. "Marian Wright Edelman," *Biography Today—Profiles of People of Interest to Young Readers* (Detroit: Omnigraphics, 1993), p. 128.

13. Woodward, pp. 185–186.

Chapter 7

1. Steve Otfinoski, *Marian Wright Edelman: Outspoken Defender of Children's Rights* (Woodbridge, Conn.: Blackbirch Press, 1991), p. 30.

2. Norman Atkins, "Marian Wright Edelman: On the Front Lines of the Battle to Save America's Children," *Rolling Stone*, December 10, 1992, p. 202.

3. Judith Viorst, "The Woman Behind the First Lady (Children's Advocate Marian Wright Edelman Influences Hillary Clinton)," *Redbook*, June 1993, p. 66.

4. Kim Hubbard, "Save the Children," *People*, July 6, 1992, p. 102.

5. Viorst, p. 66.

6. Otfinoski, p. 32.

7. Audrey Edwards, "The Fifth Essence Awards," *Essence*, May 1992, p. 78.

8. Diane Granat, "Mother Knows Best," *Washingtonian*, November 1992, p. 42.

9. Ibid.

10. Marian Wright Edelman, *The Measure of Our Success: A Letter to My Children and Yours* (Boston: Beacon Press, 1992), p. x-xi.

11. Wallace Terry, "We Don't Have a Child to Waste, an Interview with Marian Wright Edelman," *Parade*, February 14, 1993, p. 5.

12. Carol Lawson, "A Sense of Place Called Family, at Home with Marian Wright Edelman, " *The New York Times*, October 8, 1992, p. C6.

13. Edelman, p. xi.

14. Ibid.

15. Ibid, p. 28.

16. Viorst, p. 66.

17. Edelman, p. 27.

Chapter 8

1. Mickey Kaus, "The Godmother: What's Wrong with Marian Wright Edelman?" *New Republic*, February 15, 1993, p. 21.

2. Ibid.

3. Marian Wright Edelman, *The Measure of Our Success: A Letter to My Children and Yours* (Boston: Beacon Press, 1992), p. 11.

4. Wallace Terry, "We Don't Have a Child to Waste, an Interview with Marian Wright Edelman," *Parade*, February 14, 1993, p. 5.

5. "They Cannot Fend for Themselves," *Time*, March 23, 1987, p. 27.

6. Beverly Guy-Sheffall, "Marian Wright Edelman," *Notable Black American Women* (Detroit: Gale Research, 1992), p. 311.

7. Matthew S. Scott, "The Great Defender," *Black Enterprise*, May 1992, p. 67.

8. Kaus, p. 22.

9. Judith Graham, ed., "Edelman, Marian Wright," *Current Biography Yearbook, 1992* (New York: H. W. Wilson, 1992), p. 182.

10. Steve Otfinoski, *Marian Wright Edelman: Outspoken Defender of Children's Rights* (Woodbridge, Conn.: Blackbirch Press, 1991), p. 47.

11. Judith Viorst, "The Woman Behind the First Lady (Children's Advocate Marian Wright Edelman Influences Hillary Clinton)," *Redbook*, June 1993, p. 68.

12. Otfinoski, p. 47.

13. Terry, p. 5.

14. Marian Wright Edelman, "On This Mother's Day, a Message," *Parade*, May 8, 1994, p. 5.

15. Olive Wright Covington, interview with the author, National CDF Conference, March 3, 1994.

16. Lisa Shulock, interview with the author, National CDF Conference, March 4, 1994.

Chapter 9

1. Audrey Edwards, "The Fifth Essence Awards," *Essence*, May 1992, p. 78.

2. Steve Otfinoski, *Marian Wright Edelman: Outspoken Defender of Children's Rights* (Woodbridge, Conn.: Blackbirch Press, 1991), p. 55.

3. "Games Boys Play," *The Nation*, October 15, 1990, p. 404.

4. Clara Bingham, "Saint Marian," *Harper's Bazaar*, February 1993, p. 155.

5. Children's Defense Fund, *The State of America's Children Yearbook, 1992* (Washington, D.C.: Children's Defense Fund, 1992), p. xix. Reprinted by permission of Marian Wright Edelman and the CDF Staff.

6. "Hillary Clinton Reveals Black College Grad Helped Direct and Shape her Career," *Jet*, November 2, 1992, p. 6–7.

7. Ibid, p. 7.

8. Judith Viorst, "The Woman Behind the First Lady (Children's Advocate Marian Wright Edelman Influences Hillary Clinton)," *Redbook*, June 1993, p. 66.

9. Lynn Smith, "Power at Last," *Los Angeles Times*, April 7, 1993, p. E2

Chapter 10

1. *Kids Don't Have a Voice in Congress, You Do*, a pamphlet produced by Ben & Jerry's and the CDF, 1994.

2. Children's Defense Fund, *Congressional Workbook, 1994* (Washington, D.C.: Children's Defense Fund, 1994), p. 91.

3. "They Cannot Fend for Themselves," *Time*, March 23, 1987, p. 27.

4. Carol Lawson, "A Sense of Place Called Family, at Home with Marian Wright Edelman," *The New York Times*, October 8, 1992, p. C6.

5. Lynn Bowersox-Megginson, CDF director of media relations, lecture, "Are You Ready for Prime Time? Broadcast Skills Training," National CDF Conference, March 4, 1994.

6. Norman Atkins, "Marian Wright Edelman: On the Front Lines of the Battle to Save America's Children," *Rolling Stone*, December 10, 1992, p. 127.

7. "Mother Marian," *Psychology Today*, July–August 1993, p. 27.

8. Lawson, p.C6.

9. Judith Viorst, "The Woman Behind the First Lady (Children's Advocate Marian Wright Edelman Influences Hillary Clinton)," *Redbook*, June 1993, p. 68.

10. Judith Graham, ed., "Edelman, Marian Wright," *Current Biography Yearbook, 1992* (New York: H. W. Wilson, 1992), p. 182.

11. Olive Wright Covington, interview with the author, February 3, 1994.

12. Clara Bingham, "Saint Marian," *Harper's Bazaar*, February 1993, p. 157.

13. Marian Wright Edelman, *The Measure of Our Success: A Letter to My Children and Yours* (Boston: Beacon Press, 1992), p. 6.

14. Eleanor Clift, "A Mother's Guiding Message," *Newsweek*, June 8, 1992, p. 27.

Further Reading

Bullard, Sara. *Free at Last: A History of the Civil Rights Movement and Those Who Died in the Struggle.* New York: Oxford University Press, 1993.

Burch, Joann J. *Marian Wright Edelman: Children's Champion.* Brookfield, Conn.: The Millbrook Press, 1994.

Edelman, Marian Wright. *The Measure of Our Success: A Letter to My Children and Yours.* Boston: Beacon Press, 1992.

Graham, Judith, ed. "Edelman, Marian Wright." *Current Biography Yearbook, 1992.* New York: H. W. Wilson, 1992, 178–183.

Guy-Sheffall, Beverly. "Marian Wright Edelman." *Notable Black American Women.* Detroit: Gale Research, 1992.

Kallen, Stuart. *The Civil Rights Movement.* Edina, Minn.: Abdo and Daughters, 1990.

Levine, Ellen. *If You Lived at the Time of Martin Luther King.* New York: Scholastic, 1990.

"Marian Wright Edelman." *Biography Today: Profiles of People of Interest to Young Readers.* Detroit: Omnigraphics, 1993.

Otfinoski, Steve. *Marian Wright Edelman: Outspoken Defender of Children's Rights.* Woodbridge, Conn.: Blackbirch Press, 1991.

Index

A

ABC (Act for Better Child
Care), 91, 93
Abernathy, Ralph, 40
Africa, 36, 68
Anderson, Marian, 12
Atlanta, Georgia, 33, 40,
42–44

B

Baptist bar mitzvah, 71
Bennettsville, South Carolina,
12, 13, 21, 27, 28, 29,
30, 32, 36, 70, 87,
108–110
Black Codes, 22, 23
Bowersox-Megginson, Lynn,
107
boycott, 40
Brown v. *the Board of Education
of Topeka, Kansas*,
27, 29
Bush, George, 91, 94
business support for CDF,
104–105, *106*

C

Carter, Jimmy, 80, 81
CDF (Children's Defense
Fund), 75, 76–78,
80–84, *82*, 86, 87, 89,
91, 93, 94, 98, 100,
101–105, 107, *109*
Child Development Group of
Mississippi, 6, 9, 62,
63
Child Watch Visitation, 102,
103

civil rights, 13, 34, 38, 44, 50,
52, 54, 59, 62, 66, 76,
77, 81
Civil War, 22, 25
Clark, Joseph, 5, 6, 63
Clinton, Bill, 99, 100
Clinton, Hillary Rodham,
98–100
CoFo (Council of Federated
Organizations), 56
Coles, Robert, 62, 110
Congress, 9, 68, 78, 80, 81,
83, 84, 89, 93, 94, 105
CORE (Congress of Racial
Equality), 56
Covington, Olive Wright, 12,
16, *17*, 34, 36, 45, 46,
87, 108

D

desegregation, 29, 40

E

Edelman, Ezra Benjamin, 69,
72, 73, *74*, 108
Edelman, Jonah Martin, 69,
71, 72, *74*, 108
Edelman, Joshua Robert, 69,
70, 73, *74*, 107
Edelman, Marian Wright
arrested, Atlanta sit-in,
43–44
Bar exam passed, (first
African-American
woman in Mississippi),
60, 62
childhood, 10, 12–22,
25–31
children born, 69

"children's crusader," 78
Children's Defense Fund
  established, 76
college, 32–37, 43–47, 52
father's death, 27, 29
fear of bombs, 56, 58
fear of dogs, 52
France, study in, 37
law degree received, 52
marriage, 67
*The Measure of Our Success: A
  Letter to My Children and
  Yours* published, 94, 96
meditation, 108
Mississippi Summer
  Project begins (first
  job), 55
mother's death, 87
music, 13, 108
Russia, visit to, 38, *39, 41*
volunteered to help
  NAACP, 44
volunteered to help
  SNCC, 50
Washington Research
  Project established, 66
Edelman, Peter Benjamin, 6,
  9, 63, 65–69, 72, *74,*
  80, 83, 100, 107, 108

F

*Families in Peril: An Agenda
  for Social Change,* 94
France, 36

G

Gandhi, Mohandas, 42
Greenwood, Mississippi, 50,
  51, 52, *53*

H

Hatch, Orrin, 83, 93
Head Start, 59–60, 62, 80,
  84, 93, 94, 101

J

Jackson, Mississippi, 5, 52,
  54, 55, 62, 63
Jim Crow, 20, 22, 23, 25, 27,
  38, 42, 63
Johnson, Lyndon B., 59, 63

K

Kennedy, Edward (Teddy),
  81, 83
Kennedy, Robert, 5–9, *8,*
  63–69, 76
Khrushchev, Nikita, 38, *39*
King, Martin Luther, Jr., 34,
  40, 50, 66, 67, 69

L

literacy test, 49, 63
lobbyist, 78

M

*The Measure of Our Success:
  A Letter to My
  Children and Yours,*
  71, 72, 94, 96
Mississippi Summer Project,
  54–56
Montgomery, Alabama, 38, 40
Moscow, 38, 41
Moses, Robert, 50

N

NAACP (National
  Association for the
  Advancement of
  Colored People), 44,
  52, 55–58, 65
Nixon, Richard M., 69, 78
nonviolent protest, 42, 43

O

Ogata, Stella, 100
Operation Crossroads, 38

127

P

Parks, Rosa, 38
Plessy v. *Ferguson,* 23, 27
poll tax, 49
protest, 42–44

R

Reagan, Ronald, 83, 84, 91
Russia, 36, 38, 67

S

SCLC (Southern Christian
      Leadership
      Conference), 56
segregation, 19–22, 42, 43, 59
"Service is the rent you pay
      for living," 12, 101,
      110
Shalala, Donna, 100
Shiloh Baptist Church, 12,
      13, *15,* 32, 33
sit-in, 42–44, 48
SNCC (Student Nonviolent
      Coordinating
      Committee), 48, 50,
      56
South Carolina, 11, 25, 27,
      40, 63, 110
Spelman College, 32–*37,* 43,
      44, 46
*The State of America's Children
      Yearbook,* 84
Supreme Court, 23, 27, 29,
      33, 59, 63, 67, 100
Switzerland, 36

T

teen pregnancy, 77, 84, *85,*
      86, 87, 101
Truth, Sojourner, 81
"Twenty-five lessons for life,"
      96–98

U

University of Geneva,
      Switzerland, 36

V

vote, 23, 48, 49, 52, 76, 104
voter registration, 50, *51,* 55,
      56, 59
Voting Rights Act, 63

W

Washington, Booker T., 13
Washington Research Project,
      66, 68, 69, 75, 99
Wright, Arthur Jerome,
      10–14, 16, *17,* 19, 26,
      27, 29, 32
Wright Home for the Aged,
      27, *28*
Wright, Maggie Leola Bowen,
      11–14, *17,* 27, 32, 36,
      38, 43, 44, *47,* 54, 67,
      70, 87, 110

Y

Yale University, 45, 46, 52,
      98, 108

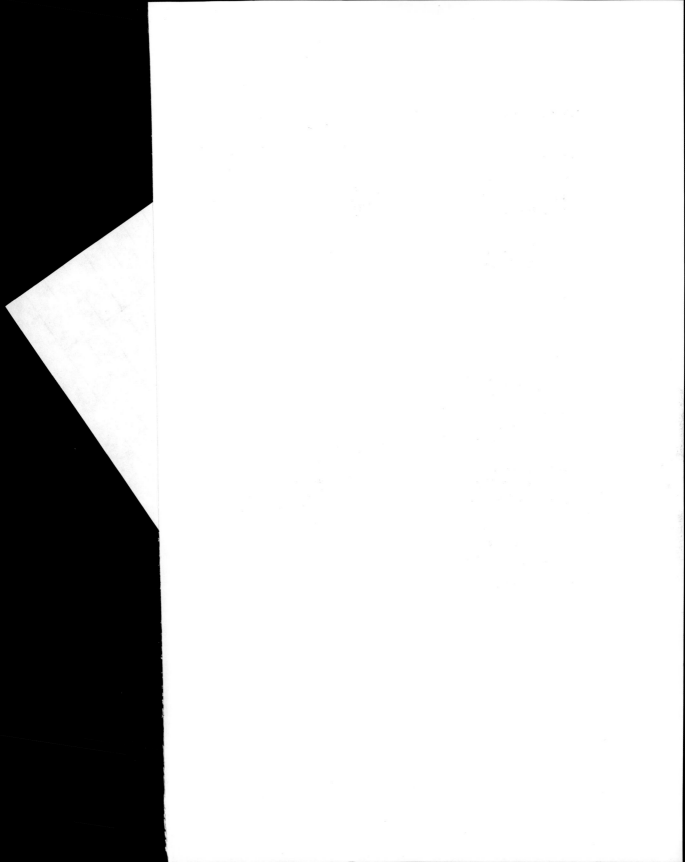

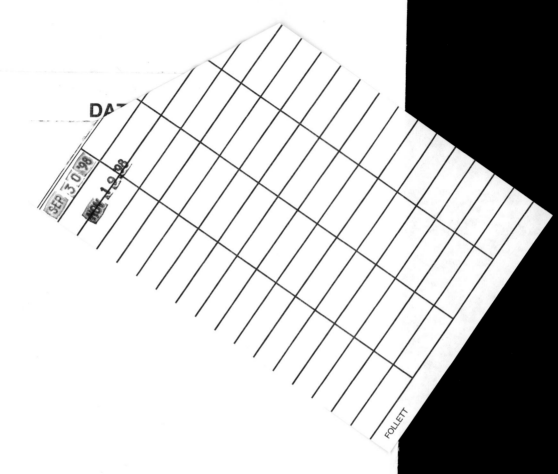